Praise for *Ask*

MW00779927

From my experience of working with Will and Chad for many years, I know firsthand that they live what they teach. This book is an anthem to Will and Chad's potent teaching, waking people up to themselves and others—for the benefit of us all.

Dr. Laurie L. Mulvey, Executive Director
World in Conversation, Center for Public Diplomacy

In a world where certainty is valued and judgment often replaces discernment, *Ask Powerful Questions* builds a compelling case for fostering curiosity, finding clarity, and creating connections. If you dare, follow the simple (but not easy) path that Will Wise provides to help you find self-awareness, empathy, and personal transformation.

Maren Showkeir, Coauthor
Authentic Conversations: Moving from Manipulation to Trust and Commitment

Listening is our most fundamental tool for healing the world's wounds and I thought I was pretty good at it. But after reading Wise and Littlefield's book, I realize that I have a long way to go. At the same time, I am excited because now I have become aware of the basics of good listening—e.g., the traps to avoid, the dispositions to cultivate, the tools to hone. Wise provides all this and more through personal stories, compelling examples and effective practices. The result: A concise treatise on the fundamentals of transformative listening.

Dr. Christopher Uhl, Author
Teaching as if Life Matters: The Promise of a New Education Culture

ASK
POWERFUL
QUESTIONS

Create
Conversations
That Matter

WiLL WiSE
CHAD LiTTLEFiELD

*To my rock, whose ability
to share so authentically and transparently
makes asking questions fun—and sometimes
a bit, just a bit, scary.
Thanks for choosing to be my wife
and life partner.*
—Will Wise

*To my son, Otto. I'm writing this sentence
just days before you are even born.
Yet, you have already ignited my curiosity.
My intention is to channel that curiosity
into our relationship, so that I get to meet
you each and every day as if it is the
first time our paths crossed.*
—Chad Littlefield

Contents

Chapter 1
Intention

Chapter 2
Rapport

Chapter 3
Openness

Chapter 4

Listening

Chapter 5

Empathy

Chapter 6

Advanced Skills

Introduction

Nothing shapes our lives so much as the questions we ask,
refuse to ask, or never dream of asking. Our minds,
bodies, feelings, and relationships are literally
informed by our questions.

— Sam Keen[1] —

This book is a result of failure.

I had failed so many times in my life that in my youth I began to create a long list of reasons why I did not fit in. No matter where I landed, my list continued to grow and I continued to land in a lot of new places. There were some years when I worked in six different states. There were other years in which I travelled around the world, looking for a place to fit in. I didn't know then what I was looking for, but in hindsight I can see it more clearly.

I am socially awkward. Fitting in is not natural for me. It has always been this way. I can't even think of a time when I have truly fit in—even as a child, I was separated from my family. Later, as an adopted member of a new family, I tried so hard to fit in that I failed to understand who I was. I didn't even know how to hug until I was in college. It was my roommate's friends who were part of an InterVarsity Christian Fellowship Club and who taught me how to hug and even what a real hug is. Then when it came time to enter the work force, I consistently landed jobs that placed me on the periphery of an experience, like when I was leading prisoners through the desert as part of a maximum security wilderness program or when I traveled to Nepal for the Peace Corps. In each case I was participating with others, but as the lone outsider looking in.

Now, with time and practice, I might make fewer social faux pas, but I can still clearly see signs of the mistakes that I make. Perhaps these challenges are a gift because they have allowed me to connect with many people in many places. Failure is common and it offers data on what is working and what is not. The intent of this book is to add something to the experience of being human that I have seen as missing.

My own social backwardness was a result of not "being seen" for so long that I was afraid of someone actually "seeing" me. It was far safer for me to blend in, to be in the shadows. If someone did see me, it was shocking and I would run. Once I made a different choice and it made all the difference.

The first "new choice" moment I recall happened in high school when I was traveling around to check out college campuses.

I was traveling north on a Greyhound bus heading to someplace that I can no longer remember, maybe to tour a college campus. I do clearly remember throwing on a cloak of invisibility, wanting to hide from the world. I peered from beneath it, watching the world go by, questioning who I was, questioning what I wanted to get from the world. Then quite suddenly, someone was shaking me out of my hiding. Not physically, though it might as well have been. It was with a simple question from one stranger to another. An Amish man said hello and asked me a question, "What's your story?" Immediately I wondered,

"How did he see me? Is he talking to me?" When I looked up into his eyes, I could see his sincere, intense curiosity. He wanted to know. When I got on the bus, I was thinking about "me." Now this man was seeing me as an equal and inviting me into his world. A world that was so much bigger than just me, and so different from my own. I chose to accept this invitation into his world and was rewarded with a fulfilling dialogue. We each learned things about the other's life. Until he said, "I'm thinking of adopting."

In that moment, the world stopped. All the cars zooming past us froze. This kid bouncing up and down in the seat behind us was suddenly still. "How did he know my secret?" The secret that I had been hiding from everyone was instantly exposed from its home in a dusty old banker's box, covered with chains, locked, and buried deep within. Even when folks said, "You look like your mom," I would smile and nod affably, but knew that she and I were not related.

Of course, when I paused, I realized that this man's remark was just happenstance and that he didn't actually know my secret. Still, in that moment, it felt like much more then pure coincidence.

He continued: "But I'm not sure if it's the right thing to do. What do you think?"

Red Alert, lights flashing, abort! I wanted to run. Or at least the old me would have run. In this moment, however, the situation was different; the Amish man saw me and I knew I needed to do something differently. I needed to share my secret for the first time with a

stranger—for no other reason than that it could be helpful
for him and some future child. I knew in that moment
that I could have an impact on how he saw the world. So
I made a new choice. I took out the banker's box, blew off
the dust, and used his question like a key to open the lock.

I took a breath (more like a gasp) and said meekly,
"Being adopted was the best thing that ever happened to
me." Long pause, another loud breath, then I continued: "It
might have even saved my life."

Our eyes connected, and I could see his fear wash
away. Like magic, the banker's box became a treasure
chest full of jewels. A gift for him, but also a gift for me.

I was no longer in a small isolated bubble. Now I was
a part of something in which we were creating something
new together, maybe a new life for a child in need, maybe
a man who wanted to be a loving father. Maybe . . . More
questions effortlessly as we explored this new space. He
was full of curiosity. His world shifted and so did mine.
Instead of getting something from the world, I suddenly
had a desire to give. To give all I had.

As I got off the bus, I was floating and found myself
saying, "Yes, Yes, YES!" I was seen, I was heard, someone
understood me, and not only knew but valued my life
experience, maybe for the first time in my life—and it felt
like a weight had been lifted. I was accepted for who I was,
and that was all that mattered.

To this day, I would love to have the chance to say "THANK YOU!"
to this man. I am deeply grateful for his choice to connect with

a random stranger while riding a bus . . . He taught me the value of connecting. Perhaps the most important lesson is that people want to be heard and understood. It may be the highest calling of our humanity.

Since that moment, I have dedicated myself to exploring ways to connect and invite "real" conversation to be a part of our normal lives. From my perspective, what is missing are questions. POWERFUL questions! Questions that allow for unscripted responses, leading us to places of the unknown. Conversations in which deep listening can happen almost effortlessly.

The Asking Powerful Questions Pyramid™

After years of working with others to teach them the importance of real conversation, I experienced another pivotal moment in my life, one which propelled me to write this book. The catalyst moment happened during a ten-day silent retreat. I was reflecting on my life, my teaching, and suddenly connections between concepts clicked. I could see clearly how I would set about sharing this knowledge about powerful questions with a larger audience. The Asking Powerful Questions Pyramid appeared. Ever since that moment, I have been sharing these concepts with folks in many different professions, from CEOs of global corporations like Mead and GE to entrepreneurs at tech start-ups. My life has not been the same since.

As we move through the text, we will start from the bottom of the Pyramid with Intention and travel upwards. The foundational skills at the lower end of the Pyramid increase your ability to work on skills further up the Pyramid. Each skill builds upon its predecessor. As you ascend, you will strengthen your ability to

With you
EMPATHY
I get you
LISTENING
I hear you
OPENNESS
I see you
RAPPORT
I am willing to know you
INTENTION

ask powerful questions in a variety of situations. Students excel when they practice a level before moving to the next level.

It is also useful to note that if you are practicing skills at a particular level and things are not working, you can diagnose the problem by stepping down the Pyramid, checking on your tools at each level and ensuring that you are fully implementing them. For example, if you are using skills on the Empathy level and are finding it difficult to connect, you revisit your Listening skills. If something still feels awry, readdress Openness. Still not working for you? Step down to Rapport. Finally, take another pass at exploring your Intention. Head backward down the Pyramid, stopping at each step and examining your tools. One exception to this procedure is the concept of intention. Intention and its tools are so foundational that you can return to this level at any time, from any other skill on the Pyramid. We will discuss this more in Chapter 1.

You might be wondering why this model is a Pyramid rather than a triangle. There are two major reasons. First, each layer has depth. It falls off the two-dimensional world into a world full of rooms, hallways, and places yet unknown. Second, there are multiple ways to describe each layer. The words Intention, Rapport, Openness, Listening, and Empathy can describe one Pyramid face. Rotate the Pyramid and you can use the following statements to describe the layers as well: I am willing to know you, I see you, I hear you, I get you, and I feel with you.

People want to be seen. They want to know that you hear them (Openness), get them (Listening), and can feel what they are feeling (Empathy). Each of the Pyramid's layers communicates a desire to make a connection—a desire to truly discover someone. Using the tools in this book, you will be able to travel through these layers of connection bravely and ask questions that will have a powerful effect.

After years of practice, failure, teaching, and studying, I now have tools to share with others that help them deal with the hard and awkward moments of life. These tools have been helpful in many different settings. I have used these concepts to train people to facilitate conversations about subjects that are often taboo, such as race and gender relations, and to help business leaders better mentor their employees in one-on-one coaching sessions. It brings me great pleasure to see people's faces light up when they discover how they can use this material in their own lives. As their ability to ask powerful questions increases, they ask more powerful questions of themselves as well. The people who really excel with this process are doing two things: asking powerful questions of others *and* asking powerful questions of themselves. This has become so habitual that I now believe the practices have become intertwined. A transformation happens for these people, as it did for me on the bus. I was questioning what I wanted to *get* from the world and I was burdened by heaviness. That weight lifted the moment I started asking how I could *give* and took the time to marvel at the world's gift of lightness. The tools in this book have been a continuous inspiration for me because of the impact they've had on others. One particularly memorable transformation I was fortunate enough to be a part of involved a former college student, Brad, who told stories of being white and growing up in a black culture. In Brad's mind, the world was "out to get him and his peers." When he spoke, his eyes would be revealed from under his hiding place—an immaculate baseball hat (complete with stickers still on it). His cheeks would turn red, his hands would turn into fists so tight that his knuckles turned white (except for the one pointing at his current victim), and the F-word was his poison. Brad was like a dangerous snake ready to strike.

He carried so much anger that it was difficult for him to learn. As an instructor intent on developing leaders, that was a problem for me. My students go through a difficult selection process to be in the class, so someone on my team must have seen something special in him, and yet it was rare that I saw anything but anger in him.

Once he learned to ask questions of himself, his life began to turn around. You can get a sense of his transformation from his communication below.

In an email he sent after the class, Brad wrote, "Before

taking this class and learning this material, I blamed the police, I blamed the school administration, I blamed the culture, but I forgot one thing—I forgot to blame myself."

Upon reflection after the class, Brad shared this post on social media. "It's painless to pretend like we are victims in this life, putting off our happiness to the circumstances presented. Is that really how you feel though? Do you really feel that helpless? If so, why? If so, what's holding you from seeing all this magic? Saying, 'It's not my fault, it's yours.' Swallow those words and smile. Take responsibility for your journey. Take pride in it. Look at you! You started as a seed, shot out a vagina, and now you're skipping around a flying spaceship through a galactic cosmos. Such a special opportunity to feel bliss in this short existence we call human. It's open for you to see, I know this, and you know this. How do we experience reality fully? Where to start? Why do we choose to read, or watch or counsel or drug ourselves, having been taught to seek only outside for answers? Why have we never been told to ask ourselves? It's not too late to start."

When Brad began this journey of asking questions, unbeknownst to him, he became an explorer. He started the journey as an expert, fully knowing how the world was and what to expect of it. When it did not go as he expected, he learned to blame everyone and everything around him. As his ability to ask powerful questions grew, he fully stepped into a new role as an explorer embracing the unknown, open to dancing with the mystery we call life. He is now having conversations that matter.

Who Is This Book For?

Are you ready to dance with the mystery? Are you ready to explore the unknown that surrounds you? We all have interactions and moments with other people that have made us wonder what the story is behind their life choices. Are you curious about what they are thinking? Curious about what is really going on? If so, then the material in this book will be useful for you.

Asking powerful questions is equally important whether you are a volunteer who runs church groups, a CEO who runs fast-paced corporate meetings, or a schoolteacher in a public school system. *Ask Powerful Questions* is useful no matter who you are, because no matter what you do, you interact with people, and everyone has a unique story to tell about who they are in the world. Each person has something valuable to share. The hard part is getting to that value: it can be like trying to open the twenty-two-ton safe door to the gold reserves at Fort Knox. Asking powerful questions will invite others to open that door and share meaningful knowledge, ideas, and thoughts. If you can ask questions that invite others to share, everyone will benefit. There is a wealth of intelligence available in the people around you and new insights to be found by asking powerful questions that will lead to a new level of collaboration and innovation.

You can be a catalyst to creating conversations that matter.

The people in your life have unique perspective. Gaining an understanding of that perspective will broaden your worldview. For instance, the CEOs of most companies became CEOs because they can solve complex problems. Solving problems requires knowledge. Most CEOs have moved so far from the "front lines" that they no longer have direct access to that knowledge. By asking powerful questions of people who have that knowledge—the front-line employees—they will be able to see complexities more completely and solve problems more effectively.

Once I was working with the CEO of a large organization. He was well practiced at solving immediate problems and delegating responsibilities. However, he was blind to his impact on those who worked for him. I observed this multiple times where people would say one thing in front of him and something else at the water cooler, while looking over their shoulder. Or, they would say one thing to me that would be useful for the CEO to know, and when I asked them if they had shared this with the boss, they would say, "Keeping your head down is the best way not to get hit by the whack-a-mole mallet." He created an atmosphere where his team told him what he wanted to hear, rather than the truth. Frankly, people were afraid of him, and it showed in all the little interactions. When I pointed this out to him, during a coaching session to discuss shifting the culture, the world stood still for a while. He realized that he only asked very narrow questions that elicited responses that were in alignment with what he was searching for, like "Why did this happen?" or "What's the problem?" rather than being open to what truly was happening within the company. He was looking for problems he could fix in a jiffy instead of long-term solutions.

Once he opened up and asked questions like, "What's working here?" or "How did I contribute to this?" his worldview expanded. It was now possible for him to really listen and help the company move forward.

The tools detailed in this book were developed to help my clients communicate with the people around them. I have facilitated professional and team development programs for large organizations and have coached their CEOs. I have also taught and facilitated students in a major university setting. I both practice and teach these tools in these settings almost daily. Before sharing these ideas, I used my own life as a testing ground filled with many refinements and, of course, failures. I have now shared this material with many students, directors, business leaders, and teachers who have responded with positive feedback about the wonderful changes in their lives. It is this success and encouragement that has empowered me to take the time to write these thoughts down and to share them. In writing this, I have been inspired by how the material continues to teach me.

Maybe failing so many times created my desire to share this work. I don't want others to feel the pain of failing as I have. I trust that this material can make the world a better place, even if it is just one question at a time.

Once during a random encounter in a campus hallway, I observed one of my former students going through the process of locking down the facility after the final facilitation course of the day. I could see she was traveling with the same cloak of invisibility I wore that day on the bus. Her face was filled with deep sadness—the kind buried so deeply that it is nearly masked by the day-to-day routine of pretending to be "fine." One look, though, and I could see she was anything but. Though she was fully covered in her Muslim appropriate attire, I could see that she had gained some pounds, her face rounder than I had ever seen it. It was late, time to go home, and yet I knew if I did not "see" her fully, I would have allowed some magic moment of awareness to slide by.

It took some courage to break the routine and ask, "What is going on for you right now?" She responded with a light answer, inviting me into the "fine" ruse she was showing the world. I responded: "What is really going on for you right now?"

Again, she tried to avoid the truth, though it was painful: "What do you mean, everything is fine?"

Smiling I said, "Okay, we can both pretend that is true, and we can leave this conversation as if LuuLuu is happy. I'm willing to do that if that's what you want. Also, I want you to know that I can see you and I see something else. It is your choice."

A big pause, a long exhale, and she looked up and said, "What do you see?"

"I'm not completely sure . . . I see what I think looks like a deep sadness. You have gained weight in the last six months, and I don't see the LuuLuu who is excited about what the world has to offer. If I had to guess, you have a big burden you are carrying that you are afraid of, and maybe afraid to share. What are you afraid of?"

LuuLuu smiled for a moment, I'm guessing because she was seen, and then immediately frowned as she told me about the deep sadness that she was encountering with her family wanting her to be someone she was not. She was not leaving her bed except to come to work (the work really mattered to her), she was stuffing her feelings with food, and she was having thoughts of suicide. Though I'm not a therapist, it sure sounded like a big case of deep depression in which she felt like she did not have any choices. Fear was holding her back.

We talked for a while. I asked her some powerful questions, to which she did not have direct answers. In turn, she asked her own questions that got me thinking, too. It was one of those deep dialogues that changes the worldview of both people. In the end, I asked her to make a promise to get some help. When I saw her next, she was choosing ways to make a difference in the world and was not hiding so much. She realized that everything she really wanted was on the other side of a wall she called fear. Questions created a doorway for her to walk through that wall of fear.

One question from me gave her the chance to choose a different way of life. One question brought two faraway worlds closer and gave permission for both people to live more fully.

Both LuuLuu and I parted that evening as fuller and more enriched versions of ourselves. It would have been easy to avoid mustering the courage to engage and, instead, offer the simple dialogue to which we've all grown accustomed: "How are you?" "Fine, thanks." Period. I saw a face and actions in LuuLuu that did not match how I expected to see the world, and I wanted to know more. A simple question opened her guarded twenty-two-ton door. We both chose to step into a world of connection and to be adventurous: we chose to *explore the unknown that surrounds us.* We chose to have a conversation that made a difference, one that mattered.

The Science of Asking Powerful Questions

We wrote this book with your mind in mind. More specifically, we wrote this book with both the right and left sides of your brain in mind. Whether you tend to be a more analytical, rational, and logical thinker or you love to eat emotions and creative storytelling for breakfast, this book is for you.

Will has infused the book with personal stories and examples from his life to make the tools we share come alive as we unpack the art of asking powerful questions. Chad complements Will's personal stories and examples with fascinating facts and nuances in neuroscience that underpin the art of asking. In the pages to follow, the art and science of asking join together to create a simple and powerful framework. When we facilitate our interactive keynotes or workshops, we often invite people to "ruthlessly misinterpret everything we say and apply it to their own context." The same invitation applies here as we dive into some of the research and data to set the stage for the book.

As humans, we are wired to connect. And we are trying to connect. On average, we spend about ten hours per day[2] "connected" through a screen. However, Sherry Turkle, researcher at MIT, reminds us of the reality that all these "sips" of online connection never actually add up to a "gulp" of human connection that can satisfy our thirst.[3]

With the rise of infinite amounts of always available information being just a click or tap away, answers have become cheap.

Cheap answers have contributed to a national curiosity deficit—as we call it. With a shortage of curiosity about each other and the world around us, our research is finding that great questions are becoming the new currency. One of our ongoing clients at a major university orientation program said it best: "Even student leaders are struggling with the question 'What do we say?' While waiting in line for food or walking between classes, 'What do we say?'"

Forget about "saying" and telling for a moment. What about asking? With the sounding board of social media, it seems we speak more in declarative or exclamatory statements and less in questions. This national curiosity deficit fuels division and separation and prevents us from building trusting, healthy connections. Let's use our mental muscles to bend our exclamation points into questions marks. Right! I mean . . . right? Questions are like keys that unlock the lifetime of ungoogleable experience we walk around with each day. Asking powerful questions opens a window into these experiences, commonalities, differences, and possible contributions or collaborations that we each carry in our minds. For example, think of a colleague that may be difficult to get along with. What might happen if you were to ask, "What brings you joy?" If we let go of assumptions just for a moment, what might we learn? After sharing this specific question in an article on our website on the power of simple questions, a reader named Claire responded with this story:

I was recently cofacilitating a session with some colleagues who I hadn't worked with before. I suggested starting our workshop with the "What brings you joy?" question.

My cofacilitators were reluctant.

They thought it might be too hard or too personal of a question for some to answer.

So I walked over to the CEO who had hired us, and said, "Would you mind? What is one thing that brought you joy today?"

He looked surprised and told a very touching story about seeing his daughter walking into school.

Then he looked at me and said, "Thank you for asking me that. It feels so good to talk about it."

Needless to say, my colleagues were convinced, and we started the workshop with the "joy" question.

It put the audience at ease, set a positive tone, allowed participants to be vulnerable with one another without feeling as much risk. And it ignited the trust process.

I find this question also primes our brains for openness, learning, and creativity.

David Whyte, a renowned English poet, once said that "no self . . . will survive a real conversation."[4] Data about how our brains respond to curiosity and questions would tend to agree. The purpose of this section of the book is to unpack a bit of that science and research.

What is the downside to *creating conversations that matter offline and in person?* There is no backspace, no "undo send," and no ability to draft a communication and consider the ramifications for a couple hours. Face-to-face, live conversation introduces us to social and emotional risk. Our brains are wired to avoid social and emotional risk in the same way we used to avoid sabertooth tigers. Neuroscientists have even found that "social pain" and physical pain activate the same regions in the brain![5] It's easier to avoid social pain or risk than it is to take the chance of connection.

But data suggests that the *reward* sitting on the other side of the social *risk* required to ask powerful questions is massive.

For the leaders and learners reading this book who want to know about the science behind the "art" of asking powerful questions, we have inserted gray conversation bubbles (like the one below), where you will find fascinating facts and nuances of neuroscience that have been researched with rigor and packaged in a digestible way.

Woven throughout the text, each conversation bubble will unpack a bit of the research that makes the Asking Powerful Questions Pyramid™ such a robust, evidence-based framework for building relationships of trust, boosting engagement, reducing prejudice, and improving performance. Now, more than ever, the world needs brain-based skills that lead to more effective communication to amplify a culture of connection, belonging, and trust. For readability, you'll find full citations for all the research at the end of the book in case you want to dive deeper.

Did you know?

Research published in the *Harvard Business Review* from the Center for Talent Innovation found that when people feel like they belong at work, they are more productive, motivated, engaged and 3.5 times more likely to contribute to their fullest potential.[6] However, only 49 percent of full-time workers[7] say that they had "a great deal of trust" in those working above and alongside them. That said . . .

1. Companies with highly effective communication practices enjoy 47 percent higher total returns[8] to shareholders compared with the firms that are least effective at communicating.

—AND—

2. Connected and engaged employees are 87 percent less likely to leave an organization.[9] This is huge when turnover costs can be as high as 100–300 percent of an employee's base salary.

As we'll continue to discover throughout the book, the impact of effective brain-based communication has far reach across companies, universities, nonprofits, schools, and community groups. How we connect matters.

One of our favorite findings comes from Google—the nearly 100,000-employee company, not just the search engine we ask to find out how far Kathmandu is from Timbuktu (5,594 miles by the way—as the crow flies).

Google internally launched a massive research study called Project Aristotle[10] in a quest to find the characteristics of the highest-performing teams. It uncovered that the number one indicator of a high-performing, innovative team is the degree of psychological safety felt within that team. This is the academic way of saying "interpersonal trust." That trust and sense of safety develops largely through social and personal connections. The tools and framework in this book were specifically designed and created to establish those social and personal connections at work—and at home.

This also aligns with eight decades of landmark research from the Harvard Study of Adult Development[11] and the role of human connection to our overall well-being. The director of this ongoing study, Dr. Waldinger, says that "people who are more socially connected to family, friends, and community are happier, healthier and live longer than people who are less well connected." Happy and healthy employees also tend to be loyal and productive employees.

The Association for Psychological Science published a study on more than 20,000 audio recordings that found that people who had more authentic, substantive conversations also tended to be happier.[12]

Creating conversations that matter isn't just fun; it's actually essential to our health and well-being.

There is a decade of research in education and learning theory that says knowledge of personal backgrounds of others leads to shortcuts for effective communication.[13] How can we access information about people's personal backgrounds? By asking. Conveniently, the rest of the book is all about asking intentional, empathetic questions that are rooted in our natural, genuine curiosity and followed up with deep listening.

To break down communication barriers and increase connection, engagement, and trust in your teams and communities, *what if we started speaking less in periods and more in question marks?*

Overview

The intention of this book is to give you the necessary tools for asking questions that will elicit fresh and new responses. This is a skill- and experience-based book that offers even the most practiced facilitator new strategies that can be applied to life immediately.

Chapters

We will start at the base of the Pyramid with *Intention (The Power of Clear Intention)*. This foundational skill allows all the other skills to work in the most effective way.

Next, we will examine *Rapport (The Power of Being Present)*. In this chapter, I will lay the groundwork for asking powerful questions by making a connection with the people around you.

Then we will look at *Openness (The Power of Being Open)*. This chapter includes creating an open mindset and the mechanics of generating powerful, open-ended questions. It will give you an opportunity to look at how you currently ask questions and provide some clear ways to ask questions that are more than just open—they are free of defensiveness and judgment.

In the following chapter, we will explore *Listening (The Power of Reflective Listening)* and the skill required for really listening to "the other," holding what another person has shared with you in a way that encourages more sharing. There is much power in telling other people as they speak that you have heard them and that, because you have heard them, you want to know more.

The most difficult concept for me to teach has been *Empathy (The Power of Connection)*, for it focuses not on what you are doing but who you are being. We will investigate the differences between empathy, sympathy, and apathy in order to learn how to apply that understanding when asking difficult questions.

Finally, I will combine all the skills shared in the book and give you tips on how to apply them in difficult situations. We will look at the power of silence and the dynamic between debate and dialogue, simple ways to build connections between others in a dialogue, how to manage overtalkers, Steering into the Curve, and finally, working with co-facilitators.

Chapter Framework

Each chapter on your path to learning to *Ask Powerful Questions* contains the following four sections:

Core Concept

Each element of the Pyramid is explained as it relates to asking powerful questions and how it builds on previous concepts. This section will also present **Traps** you may encounter, **Antidotes** you may apply to exit the traps, and **Tools** you can use in developing your skills with the core concept.

▸ **Traps** are moments where I have commonly observed students of the Core Concepts get hung up or stuck. These moments describe the tendencies people have when first practicing the Tools in this book. Traps sometimes even cause people to shut down or prevent them from being able to move forward.

▸ **Antidotes** are generally simple and straightforward approaches offered as "cures" to counteract the traps discussed. They are the *big ideas* that will help you get out of the trap. Sometimes I will jump directly to the Tool because it makes more sense in that instance.

▸ **Tools** are actions you can take to help you move forward in a way that will be useful. It is the "antidote in action," or how you can apply the ideas of the antidote immediately in your life.

An everyday way to think about these elements would be: when you have a bad cough (the Trap), the doctor might prescribe cough syrup (the Antidote), which you need to take with a spoon (the Tool).

Did you know?

As a reminder, throughout the book, you will find little gray conversation bubbles packed with **the science behind the art of asking.**

In these conversation bubbles, you will find fascinating facts and nuances in neuroscience that have been researched with rigor and packaged in a digestible way.

These sections are intended to help illuminate the data that makes the Asking Powerful Questions Pyramid™ such a robust, evidence-based framework for improving our lives, our relationships, and our organizations.

How the Core Concept Can Be Applied in Groups

This section will discuss the considerations and techniques related to how to use the chapter's concept when working in groups.

Summary of the Core Concept

The summary contains the highlights of each chapter's concept, recapped for clarity and tied together.

Self-Work for the Core Concept

The elements of communication presented here can only be completely understood through personal practice. The powerful questions you pose to others will be more powerful when you've spent time with them yourself. The self-work assignments provide example questions and suggestions for practicing and refining the skill discussed in the chapter that you can apply in your life now.

The term *Self-Work* was coined by a student in one of my classes in response to the homework assignments. He said, "This is not *homework*. It is much deeper than that. By doing these assignments, I'm working on me. It is more like *self-work*."

Welcome to the journey. I promise you that if you fully engage with this material and do the self-work assignments, you will begin to think differently and ask questions that will have a profound impact.

Let's begin!

I am willing to know you!

INTENTION

Chapter 1

Intention

Every journey begins with the first step of articulating
the intention, and then becoming the intention.

— Bryant McGill, *Voice of Reason*[14] —

The Power of Clear Intention

Let's begin with Intention.

In training thousands of people how to ask powerful questions, together we learned some simple truths. To consistently ask powerful questions, which open up new possibilities and new ways of thinking, requires a meaningful connection between the one asking and the one receiving the question. For a long time, I thought that connection was enough. Then I discovered the power of intent, a force that can propel a question directly to the heart of what matters most. Intent has become so important that it is now the foundation of asking powerful questions. You can only unlock the true potential of your questions by first being clear about the intentions you're setting forth both for yourself and in your sharing with others.

To illustrate the power of intention, here are four lines of a simple story:

A woman is lying in bed.
A man comes in the room wearing a mask.
The man cuts the woman's chest with a knife.
The woman dies.

Reread the four lines and make sure you've got the story before reading further.

Now let me ask you a simple question. What color was the man's mask? When I have asked this in a roomful of people, I've usually gotten two answers. Do you have yours?

The two colors I most often get are white (sometimes light

blue) and black. The color matters because it points to something deeper—intention.

Consider the man wearing a white mask. Who is he and what is he trying to achieve? Or if you thought of a black mask, who is he and what is he trying to achieve?

Now we have two men. One wearing a white mask, another wearing a black one. I say two because, though their actions might be the same, they are different people, and what separates them is not only the color of the mask, but also their intent. The white-masked man is a doctor who is attempting open-heart surgery, and in this case the patient dies. The black-masked man could be a "Jack the Ripper" whose intention is to kill. For both men, the actions are the same: entering the room and inserting a blade into a woman's chest. One wants life for the woman, the other wants death. Same action, different intent. Different worlds.

The world we want to create gives birth to our intent. In this story, the man's intent presented a limited number of options for why he would be in that room. The doctor was doing everything in his power to create life, and the murderer was doing everything he could to end it. What is interesting is that if the original story had included the words "doctor" or "murderer," you would have made some instant assumptions about the intent of the man. We know that a doctor's intent is to help (unless they are mentally disturbed) and that a murderer's intent is to kill. How do the "tools" in your life help you achieve what you are aiming for? How might your intent be influencing what you see around you as possible? Your situation might not be as extreme as the example above—or it might be. Regardless, your intent is the key to unlocking your potential for asking powerful questions.

The phrase "unlocking potential" became clear to me one evening as I taught others some transformative material I was learning about, which had already had a profound effect on the relationships in my own life. Through some very personal work, I'd come to discover I'd been treating people in my life in a less-than-stellar way solely for my own gain. This had been a tough reality check for me and I wanted to share with my students the tools I'd used to reach this epiphany. I walked into the room, fully prepared and excited to share this new material. I had read all the materials several times, did long intensive trainings in how to share it, had practiced delivery, and had gathered stories that would be relevant. I did everything right. That is why I was so confused when the looks on my listeners' faces were so blank. I thought, "They are not getting it." So, I got up out of my seat, spoke louder, became more animated with my appendages going in all kinds of different directions, and pushed harder on the chalkboard so that the chalk shattered. Still more blank faces. What can I do now? I asked if they were getting it. All I got in return were more blank faces. It felt like I had entered a room of empty chairs—and I was tasked with teaching to those lifeless pieces of furniture.

When the class was over, I was exhausted, and I reviewed in my head what had happened. I had the enthusiasm, the material, the sequencing—everything in my lesson plan was flawless. What did I miss? No quick answers showed up, so I went to my favorite place—the Blame Box. I blamed the students for not being prepared *(that is why they were confused), not sleeping the night before (that is why they were tired and blank), not caring about their own lives (chumps). I proceeded to stick them all inside a box and placed it up on the shelf, punctuating my actions with a "Too bad for them." As I was packing up my materials, one of my co-teachers asked me some simple questions during our debrief that shifted and unlocked my own potential.*

She asked, "Where was your focus?"

"On this material, it's great, looking at this graphic, and . . ."

She cut me off: "And when you walked in the room, who were you focused on?"

"I was making sure I had the right materials."

Again, she was quick: "And do you see any connections?"

"Ummm." Big pause. I found myself fighting to focus on what she was asking. I was about to pull down the Blame Box and start allotting everyone a fair share. Then I turned toward her, and she was looking deeply into my eyes, inviting me to be real.

"Umm . . . Connection . . . Focus. I guess I was focused on the material and wanting to get it right . . . It is hard to teach . . . Oh! I see what you are getting at. I was focused on me."

She brightened up: "Only you know! You get to measure the results yourself."

I had lots to think about that evening and spent many hours tossing in bed. I had focused on the delivery of great material, and it did not matter to me who was in the room or what they wanted in their own lives. I walked in as the expert. My intent in sharing material, no matter how impactful it was, created the very dynamic I did not want.

The following day I got a chance to live it all over again. Same room, same material, similar population of students, and a very different focus. My intent this time was to create an experience where people could have a transformative experience with the material like I did. I walked out of the room that evening with an extra skip in my step. This time around, the room had not been full of blank faces, but fully engaged ones. There were lots of good questions—questions rooted in experiences from my students' lives.

The only shift was within me. With my intent.

As a teacher, as soon as I walk into a room, my intent has a direct impact on what happens. When my intent is to share knowledge, I become the expert, and everyone else becomes objects or faces with numbers associated with them. When I walk in with the intent to create an experience in which people realize what is possible for themselves, then magic happens.

Let's get clear about intention. Intention is key to connecting and asking powerful questions, for it brings clarity to others about "where" you are coming from. Sharing your intention allows for full transparency rather than opaqueness that leaves others guessing.

What is intention?

intention |in-'ten(t)-shən| noun
1: a determination to act in a certain way
2: the healing process of a wound
From the Merriam-Webster Dictionary

Clarity of intention is about examining the story you are telling yourself and how you are communicating that story to others. Sharing your honest intention means fully understanding the following:

- what you are aiming for
- what your purpose is
- what you plan to achieve

If we can keep to our intention and share it openly and honestly, we are more likely to arrive at our destination with fewer bumps in the road.

In relationship to our work here, we should consider the second definition of "intention," the healing process of a wound, as well as the first, even though it relates to physical wounds. Many times, the emotional wounds in our relationships are based in being unclear about our intentions, and we feel torn apart in the same way skin is lacerated when we are injured. For example, you both assume you want the same thing (love) when, in reality, you want two very different things (freedom and support). As soon as we offer a clear intention, healing is possible, and the relationship moves toward a connection of trust. Restating the intention when things get tough will bring focus back to your intention (or a shared intention). The other person may not have gotten it clearly the first time, so saying it differently might be useful.

Intention is connected to purpose, and yet it is so much more than that. The root *intendere*, from Latin, suggests "to stretch," so when you make an intention, you are inviting yourself (and others) to stretch, grow and evolve toward something greater, to something purposeful.

I was introduced to the power of intention in 2010 when being trained in Authentic Conversation by Jamie and Maren Showkeir[17]. I have a habit of holding my cards close to my chest and I do not openly share what is on my mind nor what my intent is. It is a habit that has repeatedly blocked connection and has created distance between me and those I lead and work with.

Through my work with a number of companies, I have observed that in most cases, leaders are the keepers of information, knowledge is power, and that when it comes to getting ahead in the workplace, you should only share whatever knowledge is relevant to advancing your own position within the ranks. I now know that is a bunch of poppycock. The most successful leaders and facilitators are generous with their knowledge, are open, and allow others to know what motivates them.

The act of asking powerful questions needs support that will come from intention. Working on intention first allows you to begin to focus on *who you are* rather than what you do. The astounding thing is, the clearer you are about your intention, the easier it is to accomplish what you are up to.

By being clear about your intention, you allow others the choice of which game to participate in. Reflect back to LuuLuu. She shared her story with me because she could see that the game she was playing was not the one she really wanted to play. She knew that the misery she felt was something she wanted to change, and yet she could not see how that could be possible. She felt bound to her situation and did not see her choices clearly, until my intent created a different game—a game worth playing.

We spend so much time at work and with our families trying to guess what others are thinking, as if we are all getting a PhD in extrasensory perception (ESP). Imagine a world in which people are clear about the reasons for coming together during a meeting. I'm not merely suggesting agenda items, but something much deeper—being honest about what you are aiming to achieve. Consider how much time and mental effort could be placed on the task at hand and developing the relationship, rather than having to guess what another person is trying to achieve.

Intention is at the bottom of the Pyramid, for it influences every other part of the Pyramid. When you are clear about your intention with others, you are saying, "I am willing to know you."

Did you know?

The intention of being willing to know someone can save lives. A 2001 Johns Hopkins study found that when the nurses, doctors, and anesthesiologists simply shared their names, introduced themselves, and voiced concerns before an operation, the likelihood of complications and deaths fell by 35 percent.[18] Just like us, many surgeons feel they are living in a culture of "time famine," where there is too much to do in too little time.

We are suggesting that spending a brief moment to get clear on your intention can save the lives of your meetings, gatherings, and conversations.

This willingness invites others to engage honestly about what they want and what they are working toward. When the conversation has gotten nonfunctional, confusing, or people are being irrational, chances are the intention is not clear. You cannot ask a powerful question of people and expect great and fresh answers if they are mired down by trying to guess your ulterior motives. Especially if the question renders someone vulnerable, chances are that a person will be reluctant to answer without your expressed intent. The scripts playing in the background of your drama will jump up for people and will have a direct impact on the conversation, even when no one is aware of them. Possible scripts are things like, "Am I in trouble?" or "Will I get found out?"

▶ Tool: Be clear about your intention and share it

One way to deal with the scripts playing in the background is to be meticulous in expressing your intent. Reflect upon what it is that you are truly aiming for. Once, I was working with an HR professional, Kirsten, who was frustrated with the unhealthy relationship between two people for whom she was responsible. The employees were at odds with each other, finding ways to sabotage each other's work, and creating disturbances that were affecting others on the team. Meetings were rough affairs in which one of these people would storm out of the room rather than face the truth. When I asked Kirsten what her intent was in dealing with the employees, she responded, "We are now starting formal HR procedures because I want the problem to go away." Her intent, as far as I could tell, was not even clear to her. She was looking for a short-term solution and using policy as a way to fix the problem. The bottom line was she wanted the people to go away.

By asking a few questions of Kirsten, both she and I were able to see that she was missing something. I asked questions like, "What is one step that would begin to make this problem go away?" and "What is missing in the relationship, which, if it were present, would profoundly impact the situation in a positive way?" She realized that she was starting the formal HR process because she was out of tools, frustrated, and did not know what else to do. She did not really want the people to leave the organization (they were great assets), though she knew that was the most likely outcome of the process. When her intent became more clear, she felt empowered to create a new option that was not available to her before. She decided that the best course of action was to initiate a new type of conversation and asked if I could help. The four of us walked into a room and had a conversation that uncovered "ugly stuff" between the employees, some of which was more than twelve years old. Long-ago actions chock full of unclear intent had carved a rift so vast and deep that each could no longer see the contributions the other was making to the organization. Once they understood each other, they each created new intentions, and they were able to form a healthier and productive working relationship.

Being clear also means digging deeper, never settling for the first answer you get. Digging deeper means exploring what truth lies beneath the surface, beyond the rush of the present moment. Often, going deeper means zooming out and seeing the big and overall vision. Some of us need to write our intention down in order to have it well defined. For others, discovering intention is asking ourselves a question that allows for an internal dialogue that leads to a sharp and focused vision, such as, "What am I aiming to achieve here, and what about that is important?" After posing a question to yourself, simply sit with your answer in silence and ask, "What else is there?" Often, there is something else—another buried answer or motivation—and then something deeper still. This exercise is especially useful for me if my first response is all about me or about a *need* to be right. That is fear in disguise. Often a clear (and useful) intention statement contains the needs of the other person, as well as my own needs.

Getting clear about intent is not always easy, and when the pressure is on, I can feel lost about where to begin. Sometimes, it is useful to have more direction when it comes to gaining clarity. I have found that intention can be focused in three ways (though I'm sure there are more than three, these have been the most useful):

Future-Focused: Your intention is about how you want the world to exist. ("I want to work in a place in which we all get along and can still challenge each other to do our best work.")

Outcome-Focused: Your intention is dictated by the intended results. ("When this meeting is over, I want to understand the challenges you have been facing with this project and what we can do to make it work for all of us.")

Commitment-Focused: Your intention is about promises you are making now or have made in the past. ("I love you; I want you to know that and want to understand what is getting in the way of us having a loving relationship.")

When I cannot pinpoint my intention, or I need to do so quickly (i.e., I'm in a room filled with folks who expect an immediate response from me), I use one of these three lenses to get moving in a direction. In the end, I might come up with an intent that does not clearly fit into one of these lenses, and that is okay.

I might ask myself one of these guiding questions, based on the focus I choose:

- *Future:* How do I want the world to exist?
- *Outcome:* What result am I expecting from this meeting that would be useful for everyone involved?
- *Commitment:* What promise have I made that I want to live fully in this moment?

Use these questions and others specific to your circumstance to discover what your true intent is. Once you determine what your intention is (and maybe even the motivation behind it) and can state it in a sentence (or maybe two), then you need to share it. And how do you know when to share? At the beginning of each endeavor—at the start of a meeting, for example. Did you notice that I shared my intention for this book in the very first line of the overview?

Another instance in which it's useful to state (or restate) your intention is anytime things are tough, ugly, or sensitive. When things get tough, it's easy for emotional wounds to form and for people to assume what the other's intent is. By restating your intention, it often acts as a dialogue "reset." For a moment, people can zoom out and see the big picture or the grander vision and connect the current tension that created the "tough" spot to the overall intention.

The tension doesn't go away, but its context gets shifted enough that the conversation is able to move forward in a productive way.

▶ Trap: Intention based on fear

A common place where people get stuck while attempting to get clear about their intention is when they name an intention based on fear (or an intention that is focused on oneself). If your intention is to find a way to feel safe because you feel threatened or finding a way to make yourself look good, I invite you to examine this closely. Is your intention based on fear? Do you catch yourself thinking there's not enough love or opportunities or like some force will come and slap you down if you attempt to stray from your path of safety? If that is the case, your intention isn't useful to you or those around you. In order to make meaningful connections and ask powerful questions, your desire must be to *thrive* rather than *survive*. Fear-based intentions might be perfect if you actually are in survival mode; however, if you have time to read this book, that's probably a good indication that most of your survival needs are taken care of. Choose to thrive rather than merely survive, and create an intention that is uplifting, an intention that inspires you and those around you. Intentions that move the world are intentions that enliven, rejuvenate, and exhilarate.

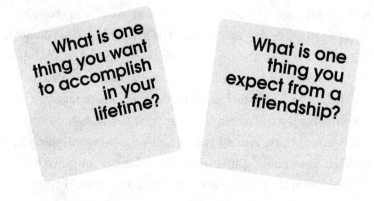

What is one thing you want to accomplish in your lifetime?

What is one thing you expect from a friendship?

▶ Antidote: Intention based on love

Be honest about what your intention is. Get to the core of it. What is it that you are aiming to achieve *for the whole*? "The whole" includes everyone and everything that you are connected to. Even if fear is present, there is usually something deeper motivating you—though hidden by fear, it is likely coming from a place of love. Like Grandma yanking the youngster away from the hot stove, both fear and love are present.

▶ Tool: Ask clarifying "we" questions

Answering some of the following questions might help you find the love in your intention:

- ▶ What is it we are trying to understand that we're unable to grasp?
- ▶ What are we trying to create?
- ▶ What will it look like if we achieve our purpose?

Answering these types of questions honestly before (and sometimes while) working with people gives us the possibility to create something worthwhile that everyone can be invested in. Did you notice the words "we" in the questions above? Often great intentions that enliven, rejuvenate, and exhilarate those around you include "we" language. Using inclusive language will encourage you to be accountable for the whole (not just your needs, but also include the needs of those around you). In this way, you will discourage yourself from holding an intention based upon your own fear.

For example, a fear-based intention might be: "I want to fix my financial situation at work." Flipping it into "we" language might be: "I intend to create a workplace that is supportive of all *our* needs, be it related to finances, health, or wellbeing."

"I intend to find a partner because I don't want to be alone" might become "I intend to create moments worth remembering in which everyone belongs."

Did you know?

Even one word can completely shift your intention to include the needs of the whole. Founders of The World Café and expert questioners, Juniata Brown and David Isaacs articulate the power of a shift in intention beautifully in their book.[19] They describe a dialogue between leaders:

> The head of Hewlett-Packard Labs was working on a global effort to realize the vision behind this question: how can we be the best industrial research lab in the world?

> While productivity was improving rapidly, something was missing. During an informal conversation, one of the lab engineers spoke up. She said, "What would get me out of bed in the morning would be to become the best for the world." Suddenly a really big question had emerged.[20]

Best *in* the world. Competition. Best *for* the world. Contribution. One *word* completely changed their *world*.

In writing the book, we actually tracked down and called one of these senior engineers to discover the impact that this had on the company. He shared with us that he took the "for the world" intention and created an image of what that meant to him. It was a well-known picture of the founders of HP looking into the backyard garage where the company began. He added a beautiful photo of Earth placed inside. This picture became the symbol of "HP for the World." The "HP for the World" image spread throughout the company—appearing in lobbies, featured in recruiting brochures, and offered as executive gifts. More than 90,000 posters were purchased by HP employees and others around the world, stimulating a growing network of conversations about the big question: how can we be the best industrial research lab *for* the world?

What made this question so powerful? We would argue that it was the *intention* underlying the question.

▶ Trap: Manipulation

Sometimes when we first try to be clear about our intentions we fake it or decide not to share an intention at all. This leaves us in a place of manipulation. Manipulation is making someone do something without ever telling them what it is you want them to do. You ask questions with a secretly expected outcome that only you are aware of. The manipulative intent is to get something from that person without directly telling them what you want. Here is an example of manipulation from one of my workshops:

> I say: "When we are done at six p.m. there is a group of old ladies who need to come in to use this space. I don't know how I will get the room set up in time for their meeting." Almost without fail someone says, "I can stay and help," and then others jump in, offering to help as well.
>
> I have gotten people to set up the room without explicitly asking them to do so. Score one for me—or so I used to think. I was never aware that I had just manipulated a group of people to do my bidding. Even adding "old ladies" and other language for the perfect "effect" contributed to the manipulation.
>
> Now that I have a better understanding of intention, I can offer a clear request. "Folks, I intend to maximize the time we have together. Another group is scheduled to use this room at six p.m. I have agreed that the room would be reset to their liking. Who would be willing to help me do that at 5:50 so we can be done by six p.m. and they can start their meeting? The other option is we finish earlier and I reset the room." Looking around the room,

if I see a number of hands I can say, "Great, that looks like enough people, so we won't have to end any earlier then 5:50. Thank you."

If, on the other hand, I look around the room and see no hands, I need to be okay with that. In that case, I might say, "Looks like we will need to end at 5:40 so I will have time to move the tables."

▶ Antidote: Be clear, true, and complete

The antidote to a world of manipulation is to have a clear intention and share it. When everyone understands your intent, manipulation no longer exists. In order for others to understand your intention, though, you must avoid faking it by making something up that you think they would like to hear and omitting the truth, in part or in whole. A hidden agenda will only create more space between you and others. On some level, they will know you're holding back. Being clear opens up the possibility for the relationship to be transparent rather than opaque. Opaqueness continues the cycle of the "guessing game" and does not lead to connection.

▶ Tool: Take the risk and share

Being clear about your intention forces you to be vulnerable, as you are now placing all your cards on the table. This may feel like a significant risk. This is scary for some of us.

In the room setup anecdote I shared above, I needed to ask for help. Asking for help does not come naturally for me; it is hard and still can be scary, even after years of practice. It is much easier to go about my business and "hope" that others will follow my lead. However, the payoff for vulnerability is always worth the risk. It is real and it creates more realness. I'm not saying it is easy. I'm saying that it pays a dividend that, with reflection, makes me say, "That was worth it." When I ask for help to get the room set up, it can happen so much faster than by doing it myself or by manipulating a few into the process. People actually want to help when given the choice; they just need to be asked or given clear directions.

When being clear about your intention you may find yourself being vulnerable because you are stating your purpose, your aim, and your plan with such rawness that you might be concerned about how people could judge it (and therefore judge you). It is a risk. I have found that it is worth the risk because now I have people around me who are agreeing to play the same game or make a difference in a similar enough way that we are on the same team. The intention unites us. Those who choose not to play are free to go and find another game that is more worthwhile for them. As a result, I don't spend my time trying to convince, sell, or defend the game I say is worthy. When you are vulnerable, you invite others to be vulnerable.

How does intention relate to asking questions? When you need to ask a tough question, it can be helpful to restate your intention so you can remind people of the game that's being played and the ultimate shared goal. The assumption that you hold a hidden agenda by posing the question is now addressed directly and with clarity.

Let's say you're in a meeting and Abby says, "I'm confused,

what is the purpose of this additional project? Our clients have not asked for this." Can you see that if someone says this, they might be unclear about the intention or purpose of the meeting or project? Restating your intention at this moment can create clearness for everyone in the room. "Abby, I would like to ask you a question. My intention in asking is to bring some clarity to everyone about the purpose of this project. Can you tell us more about what might be contributing to your confusion? I think it might give us all an opportunity to see a gap we might be missing."

If instead you say, "Why are you confused, Abby?" you will be going back in time and she will need to defend her statement. If you ask, "What has our client asked for then, Abby?" everyone will listen to Abby's view, which may not contribute to the dialogue. However, by kindly asking a question to understand her perspective, while expressing your own intention, you allow her to share in a way that is not simply her defending her views or those of the client. It allows for the possibility that she can share from a perspective beneficial to all the stakeholders and permit others to do the same. Not only have you sought to understand and express your own intention clearly, but you have also focused on the whole—the group's intention—by seeking to understand what Abby's motivation is for asking her question.

Another coaching scenario where clear intention comes in handy is when I work with executives. Inevitably, there's a place we get stuck and it usually happens right after a question is posed that they don't have an immediate answer for. The question forces them to think *newly* about a problem that has existed for years. This new thinking can be scary, so a common response is to tell stories about why the problem exists. This is a moment in which

I can pause the story and say, "My intention here is to invite you to think about this in a new and fresh way, leaving behind this stuck place we are in right now. We agreed earlier that this would require some work and maybe discomfort. This is one of those moments. Take time to think about my question in silence before responding. Would you like me to repeat the question?" Repeating my intention brings clarity to the present moment and gets us right back on track. It also allows me to work powerfully with people who have lots of power. It's clear I'm not trying to "take" or "use" their power, just have them maximize their own.

▶ Tool: Create an initial intent

One last tool before we leave intention. It is helpful if you can create an Initial Intent that can give you direction in your life when the unexpected moments show up. I was working with a new CEO of a large organization, Chris, who was feeling lost. He was getting overwhelmed with all that he had to do, and his ability to build relationships was suffering.

Chris was a "doer" and his task list was long, causing him to work twelve- to fourteen-hour days, seven days a week. In fact, he was so task-oriented that it was difficult for people to approach him out of fear they'd be "interrupting" him. After striking up a conversation with an employee in the hallway on the way to the restroom one day, Chris realized how little he actually knew about the people he was leading and realized he wanted to make more of an effort to get to know them. He wanted to change that. Together we created an Initial Intent statement that he could lean on in moments like this. His intention was: "Empowering those I lead, by knowing those I lead." Now, every time he has a surprise encounter, he has a reason to learn about what motivates those he serves. Over time, Chris got better at turning those little surprise moments into moments of connection, even though that was not his natural inclination.

Your Initial Intent could be something as simple as, "I'm curious to know what makes people tick." It does not need to be complicated. It does need to be something that you can lean on regardless of the situation. Here are a few examples:

▸ I intend to shift my conversations so that I'm not listening to win, to interject, or to prove something but to listen to understand.
▸ I intend to create a peaceful community.
▸ I intend to live in a world where everyone belongs.

Your statement should reflect what drives you, no matter what you are doing. Create a statement that you can lean on even when you are surprised at what shows up. You'll be able to cultivate more serendipitous moments that benefit everyone.

How Intention Can Be Applied in Groups

Being clear about your intent is valuable whether you're in a group or one-on-one. In a large group, it is more likely someone will not understand your intent or think you have alternative motives. I have found that it is useful to restate my intent several times in different ways. It is also useful to restate your intent before you ask the group to do something.

A second important quality is to have alignment with your

actions and your intent. Merely stating your intent might not be enough for people to get it. You will need to show them as well.

> *I was one of several leaders in a group recently meeting in a room where we have met a half a dozen times. One of the leaders made it clear that she wanted folks to be comfortable in the space. She noticed that one of the participants was rubbing her eyes. She asked about it and the participant responded, "It is nothing, my eyes hurt from working too hard and staring at a screen all day." Without missing a beat, the leader got up and dimmed the fluorescent lights in the room and asked, "Does this help?" The participant responded, "Wow, I did not know you could do that. Thank you." Her actions matched her stated intent and as a result she built trust with everyone in the room.*

Examples of group intentions:

- ‣ I intend to create a space in which all of us can find meaning in our work and make a make a difference by contributing to the whole.
- ‣ I intend that while we are working together we can support each other in such a way that lifts each of us up to be the best we can be.

You may find it useful to revisit your intention from time to time while working with a group. You'll be able to evaluate whether you are achieving your goal or are communicating your motivation adequately. Ask yourself, "What am I doing to contribute to the group's dynamic?" The group's actions and interactions will reveal whether or not you have expressed your intention well enough.

This question will also be useful for you to ask as you journey through the tools in this book. You will discover more and more ways you can positively contribute to your group's dynamic (and diagnose places where you may have contributed in unwanted ways).

You can also communicate intention to the group you're working with by addressing their experience while they're in the room with you. Ask yourself before you arrive: "What can I do to make people feel comfortable?" Food and water are simple elements that can help you create a comfortable atmosphere. Generally speaking, for most events lasting longer than two hours, participants have an expectation that beverages will be

available (at least water). If you are running a program lasting more than four hours, it helps if people have access to food. Take care of whatever participant needs you can. Giving them good food is an easy way to show you care.

You might take a few minutes to center yourself before participants arrive, so that you have a moment to rejuvenate and refocus on the intention—yours and the group's—for the meeting or event. Take a few minutes to relax and do something that energizes you.

> *If I can, I take that time outside and do a little wandering and moving around without purpose. I look for beautiful things and walk toward them: a leaf that moves to its own drum during the slightest breeze, sunlight glimmering on a drop of water, a tree standing alone amongst the craziness of the human world of movement. The beauty helps me define my purpose and reminds me of the good in the world. This is a little booster shot, especially if I will be doing some intense work (e.g., conflict resolution).*

Stay in the present moment. Greet each person as if they matter, because they do. These small details will show people that you are willing to know them and allow them into your intention. To follow through, finish your session by letting participants know what you've learned from them. Aim to create a positive experience with a group in which they feel safe enough to be themselves. You'll be able to witness how your actions contribute to the way the group functions together.

Summary of Intention

Being clear about what you intend, and sharing it, is a simple yet powerful way to be fully present in the relationships in your life. Be clear, true, whole, complete, and based in love. The result will be fewer guessing games, and you will get more done and make deeper connections.

Did you know?

Long before the neuroscience research or HP Labs case study referenced earlier in the chapter, ancient Sanskrit texts known as the Upanishads, which were written between 500 and 800 BCE, read, "You are what your deepest desire is. As is your desire, so is your intention. As is your intention, so is your will. As is your will, so is your deed. As is your deed, so is your destiny."[21]

Bringing us to the present moment, Oprah recently said this in an interview: "Intention is the principle by which I rule every action in my life." Later in the interview, she shared that "[she] used to have the disease to please and *intention* cured [her]."[22]

The power of intention is not a novel concept, but its far-reaching impacts have certainly stood the test of time.

You can access more free resources and a behind-the-scenes video from us on the power of clear intention at ***www.weand.me/intention***.

Self-Work for Intention

Before your next meeting or conversation, spend some time discovering what your intention is: your personal intention *and* your group's intention. You might ask yourself:

- What are we aiming to achieve and what about that is important for everyone?
- What is the overall picture that needs to be clear for us to fully leverage our time in this meeting?
- How can I be accountable for the whole?

When you arrive at the meeting or start the conversation, state what your intention is. Destroy the assumption that they know what your intention is by simply saying it. If the focus becomes unclear, or if things get heated at any point during the meeting, pause the conversation and return to stating the intention (maybe try using different words this time). After applying these tactics in three separate meetings, reflect upon those meetings and conversations—see if you notice a difference in how they went compared to how they usually go.

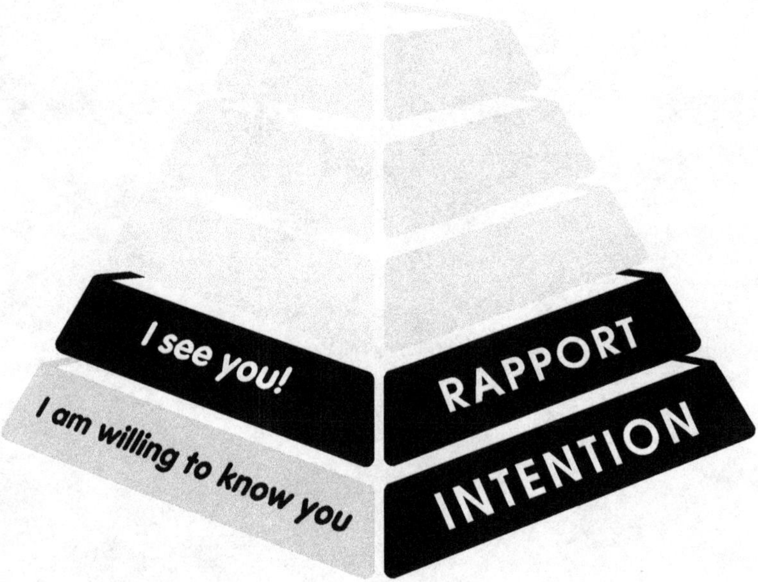
I see you!
RAPPORT
I am willing to know you
INTENTION

Chapter 2

Rapport

I define connection as the energy that exists between
people when they feel seen, heard, and valued; when they
can give and receive without judgment; and when they derive
sustenance and strength from the relationship.

— Brené Brown[23] —

The Power of Being Present

What is Rapport?

rapport |raˈpôr; rə-| noun
a close and harmonious relationship in which the people or groups concerned understand each other's feelings or ideas and communicate well: *she was able to establish a good rapport with the children | there was little rapport between them.*
ORIGIN mid-17th cent.: French, from **rapporter "bring back"**
From the New Oxford American Dictionary

Can you remember a time when you met someone new and "hit it off" right away or felt like you had known this person for a long time? The two of you just clicked.

It happens at the most unexpected places for me: on the train, on the bus, on the plane, at a party, while waiting in line. About twenty years ago, I received an unexpected invitation to connect while in a flight.

I had just settled into my seat when a woman twenty years my senior said, "Hello." I was surprised at her willingness to connect. We began a conversation that flowed as if we were old friends. I discovered that her passion was pottery, and I became so absorbed in the conversation that the hours flew by. I was full of wonder about the process of making clay into pots, and I learned about a unique glazing that no one else was using that created interesting textures and colors. It was like I was "in" on a family secret. Her passion was contagious. When the flight was over, I was left with a desire to see what was unique about how she created her pots. As we were disembarking she called out, "You have my card. Come and visit while you are in town. Really!" And later that week I did just that. The shapes and textures of the hand-thrown pottery in her studio were something I'd never seen before, and I was impressed. So impressed that I figured out how to send one to my mom through international mail. What happened between the potter and me was effortless, fun, and fully engaging. In hindsight, I can see that what connected us was our natural, genuine curiosity about who this other person was in the world.

How do moments like this happen? This book is designed to help us find ways that we can contribute to a world in which these connections happen more often.

What makes connecting with others so hard and yet so delicious when it happens? I know some people who make connecting with others look easy. What is it about them that makes it appear effortless? For me, connecting with others is a choice and it is work. It's rare that it happens without any effort on my part. Honestly, I could be in a room full of people and remain disconnected unless I make such a choice. I'm constantly generating reasons why I shouldn't connect with this person or why that person would not want to connect with me.

It is easy for me to come to work and focus on what needs to be done and allow all the relationships and people present to get "in the way" of getting my work done. It's also easy for me to justify my choice, saying to myself, "I have important work to do and I can connect with them later."

Yet often, I cannot "really" get my work done without these people. I can move some things in the right direction, I can set things up for success, but ultimately, the people around me are part of my work in some way. When I connect with them, the work flows with much more ease than when I don't connect. They offer a suggestion I could not see, or they offer me support with a simple head nod.

Did you know?

Google's quest to build the perfect team uncovered that the number one indicator of a high-performing, innovative team is the degree of psychological safety in that group. This is really the academic, PhD word for "interpersonal trust," which develops largely through social connections.[24]

In this chapter, we define rapport as "creating a relationship of trust." Through our work speaking, training, coaching, and mentoring organizations, we too have found that establishing "connection before content" and building relationships of trust creates shortcuts to more effective communication.[25]

We suggest that oftentimes the root to these communication shortcuts and relationships of trust starts by following our natural, genuine curiosity. Experience is the greatest teacher, though, so, by all means, utilize the tools in this chapter to build more trusting relationships and collect your own research on the impact of your curiosity.

This brings us to the delicious part. When I am connected with those around me, I am connected with something much bigger than myself. Their fears and desires are equal to mine, and yet, in some way, I am not burdened by them but actually uplifted. Knowing their fears, knowing their desires, and "getting them" results in moving our work forward in meaningful ways that lift all of us to the greater good. Like a great meal, it becomes a full-body experience. Something that you smell, taste, touch, see, and hear. Something that is so present that it exists only in the now.

The endeavor of asking meaningful questions starts with intention and connection. Connecting with people is fundamental to asking a powerful question. Connecting arises before you even ask a question and continues throughout your time with a client, student, parishioner, coworker, etc. It is my belief and experience that if you establish a connection with someone, then they will respond to your powerful questions more honestly and freely. Even other communications will be better received if you have established an authentic connection.

What is the process of how you connect with other people, including strangers? We have now come to the second level of the Pyramid, *Rapport*. For some of you, the word "rapport" might have some bad juju associated with it. If you do a Google search on "rapport building," you will get many hits on manipulative tricks for increasing your odds of having sex or increasing your sales success. I learned (and taught others) those tricks because I thought that they would help me start relationships. However, I ultimately came to know that these "tricks" built relationships that were fake. When there was real work to be done, the relationships failed to have enough substance to create collaboratively. In this book, the goal is to avoid these sneaky tactics disguised as shortcuts to successful relationships.

Here, the intention is to build connections that matter so that each of us can do the work we were meant to do. It will require us to take risks and to be vulnerable, and the reward will be new and fulfilling conversations.

I would suggest that rapport means building a relationship of trust or moving toward trust. Although rapport is a noun, *Rapport Building* takes a certain amount of work. It takes action. We will examine steps you can consciously take to create rapport.

But there's another element to rapport that is harder to describe. It is in those moments when we see the other person as they are. Somehow, we are open to their humanity, their fears, and their dreams.

The person is NOT:

▸ in the way or someone who you need to work around
▸ a key player to get something from
▸ someone that we're trying to impress

They just are. When you experience a moment of rapport with another person, you each feel safe in being yourselves. This allows you both to be fully present. When that occurs, it brings me joy that this person is present with me in that moment. Their eyes have that "shining" (a little extra gloss that happens to eyes when you are experiencing something that is real and heartfelt) that you see when you are truly connected. My intention is clear of any needs or desires other than the desire to connect with another person. It's not coming from a place of loneliness but a place of sheer curiosity. What would your work be like if that could happen more regularly?

What happens during those magic moments (like the one I experienced with the potter) to make people feel connected—moments in which trust is present? Each person makes a choice to be totally present with the other person and does not allow their fears to control the conversation.

▶ Trap: The fears

Our objective is to remove all the barriers to establishing rapport. Most barriers to human connection are based in fear. People commonly name two fears that are barriers in the way of connecting with others. First is the **Fear of Being Unloved**, also referred to as the Fear of Being Rejected. It is often camouflaged as not being accepted or unliked. People in my classes will frequently say things like, "I'm afraid that if I take a step toward connection, the other person may not take that step." Then thoughts arise, like, "I'm not going to be accepted," or "I am not going to be liked."

The second named fear is closely related to the first: **Fear of Looking Stupid**. By attempting to make a connection, people fear being judged. They say things like, "I may do something that is abnormal and then I will look stupid to the person that I'm trying to connect with." I'm sure we could list hundreds of additional fears here, but it's possible they are all offspring of these two. They are all real fears, and we could be in therapy for years addressing all of them—or we could simply do two things: first name the fear and then find an antidote.

Allow yourself to be brave and name the fear (however you want to refer to it). This will give you the ability to face it head-on and the opportunity to begin understanding it. So often, we let fear steer us, as if we have a nameless, invisible companion whose hands are on our shoulders, whose job it is to steer us away from the very things that we really want to do. Once you name the fear, you can acknowledge it, be thankful for its counsel, and then you can make a choice to lean into it by using the antidote.

What is one thing or situation that scares you?

What things hold you back from doing what you really want to do?

▶ Antidote: Follow your curiosity

Whatever happens, follow your natural, genuine curiosity! In whichever form fear shows up for you, your natural, genuine curiosity is a doorway, an invitation to get to know someone. Be full of wonder. Ask the questions that naturally occur for you from this place of wonderment rather than allowing fear to bury them. Your curiosity is rarely wrong, though we may tell ourselves that it is. If it is natural, genuine curiosity and you act on it, you take a step toward knowing another person. If you try to fake it, others will know and you will not be in a place of connection. It is important to act on natural, genuine curiosity. This bears repeating. Make it a mantra.

Natural, genuine curiosity is a skill you can develop by:

1. Being present.

   ▸ Slow down the desire to rush.
   ▸ Engage with what "is."

2. Paying attention to what is happening right now.

   ▸ Notice color, shape, texture. Notice tone, tempo, speed.
   ▸ Let go of what you would like it (or she/or he) to be or even what could be or should be.
   ▸ As best you can, suspend judgment or your idea of how it is.

3. Listening with your heart and your mind to what you are drawn toward.

   ▸ Let yourself be drawn toward it or them. Release the thoughts that pull you away.

4. Engaging with whatever thing or person you are curious about and discovering if there is more to be curious about.

▸ Trap: Finding commonalities

When we meet new people, we believe we need to find things in common. We are taught to believe that if we find things in common, we can build a relationship of trust. I believe this is false. We all know people who are similar to us but with whom we don't necessarily jive.

When my wife was pregnant with our first child, she was
introduced to another woman who was also pregnant.
On paper, these two should have hit it off. My wife and this
other woman were both yoga instructors, they both liked
to cook, and they both had an interest in natural birthing.
The reality was that despite how much they learned about
their commonalities, they were not able to connect.

We all know people who are quite different from us, as well, with whom we do connect. Some of my best friends are from different cultures: we seemingly have nothing in common, and yet we are kindred spirits.

Often when I use the word "connections," people seem to think I mean "commonalities." It is as if our nature is to find commonalties in order to be connected. I think this assumption is false. There are lots of ways that we can be connected and have very little in common. There can be connections around a topic, idea, or thought, and people may stand on opposing sides. That is still a connection. One person may feel that gas drilling (fracking) is wrong, while someone else may feel it is the only way toward energy independence. In a dialogue, there is a connection point around fracking, even if people think about it differently. What the connection point is, however, will be unclear till both make a choice to connect and explore possibilities together.

In general, when searching for commonalities with another person, we start broadly to find things we have in common and then we try to hone in.

I met someone recently who asked, "Where are you from?"
When I told her, she searched her mental database to find
a connection with that place and told me about a long-lost
friend who now lives there. I was left thinking: How should
I proceed? I have been taught that I should listen for a
connection I might have with this friend of hers and then
name another connection. If I don't have one, I should try to
ask questions to find a connection. If it is a dead end, then we
have to start again, stay in the awkward moment, or leave.

There is nothing inherently wrong with this approach, other than that it can take a long time (even as long as a lifetime) to really connect and find enough in common to have rapport. Yes, sometimes it can happen quickly. If that is true for you, then go ahead, use it. It can be one tool in the toolbox.

One challenge is connecting with someone with whom you do not have many obvious things in common. Another challenge is not having much time to connect with someone before you need to work together. The key is to find your natural, genuine curiosity, even when someone seems different from you. Be full of wonder:

▸ How did she get this way?
▸ How is she living that life that is so different from mine?

Act as if you are exploring unknown territory and are expecting the unexpected. Who knows what will happen next? Who knows who this person is? I can guarantee they are not who you "think" they are. They are not all the assumptions that you've made about them. They are full of dreams, hopes, and ideas.

- How did they form these?
- What experiences influenced who they are?

Let's suppose you have a meeting with someone you don't know, and she comes through the door wearing a large purple hat. It makes you smile. Your first thought is, "How do people respond to her with that hat?" You say, "Hello" and introduce yourself. You want to ask about the hat but decide not to, fearing that you will be perceived as being too forward. You tell yourself it would be much too personal and you know that you would NEVER wear a purple hat, so you assume that this is something you do not have in common. Instead, you choose to talk about something "safe" like the weather. I suggest that, on an underlying level, you've just succeeded in telling this person, "I don't see you." Your desire to find something "safe" to talk about resulted in building a relationship that is less real. You allowed a barrier to establishing rapport (Fear of Looking Stupid perhaps) to get in the way of making a true connection. You played it safe, and as a result, you did not create rapport with this person. You allowed your fears to decide how this relationship is going to be, and this will have an effect on how she interacts with you. Later, when you need to ask a tough question, she may not be as receptive. You have made a choice to base your relationship on fear, making it easier for her to make that same choice as well.

Let's look at how this could play out differently if you took the antidote and followed your natural, genuine curiosity. When you saw the hat, it made you smile. A quick question came to you: "How do people respond to her with that hat?" You say, "Hello" and introduce yourself. This is the point where you "pick up the antidote," make a choice to move toward trust, and follow your natural, genuine curiosity. You feel the risk in that choice and yet you decide that the risk is worthwhile. You choose to go for it. You say, "I'm curious about your hat. How does the world respond to you when you wear that hat?" Now that you made a choice for closeness, she can choose to do the same (or not), but you have invited her to be real and present with you. You have also demonstrated a willingness to be honest, vulnerable, and genuine. This sets a huge precedent early on in your relationship. It lays the groundwork for her to reciprocate and tells her that it is okay to have a real and meaningful relationship with you. You are telling her on a deep level that you "see" her and are willing to engage in a way that is real. It is possible that she might not reciprocate, but you are only in charge of you. You have extended the invitation and have done what you can to invite authenticity into the relationship.

▶ Tool: Ask your curiosity

Find something the person is wearing, carrying, or sharing that you are genuinely curious about and ask an open-ended question, just like in the purple hat story above. Let your wonder fill the room and follow your curiosity.

Let's say you are about to meet this man for the first time. You know his name is Jake and you are going to do some work together. As you walk closer, this is who you see.

What are you curious about? Quick, without lots of thinking, just look closely and what comes up for you? Unfiltered—we can filter later. What do you notice that you wonder about? Can you turn that into a question that you could ask him?

Give it a go. You will find it useful to practice before you read below. No one will know but you. Give yourself permission to be completely curious with the man in this photo. It will be useful for you to see your thoughts.

> "Hello. You must be Jake. I'm Will. Good to finally meet you face to face."

The first thing that jumps at me is his smile. So I could ask:

> "What is it that makes you smile so big, Jake?"
> "What's bringing you joy, Jake?"
> "Seems like you are happy about something. What's that?"

And his glasses. I'm curious about those, so I could ask:

> "I'm new to glasses and don't love these that I'm wearing. I look in the space between the lenses and my cheek because they raise up too high. How do those work for you?"

And his beard.

> "Growing it (while pointing to my beard) or going for the shadow look?"

And the plant.

> While pointing to the plant, "Got a bit of a green thumb do ya?"

And his shirt looks like it's really comfortable:

> "What's the story with that comfy shirt?"

▶ Trap: Your invisible list

When people first start using this tool, it can be easy to fall into the trap of simply asking an open-ended question about something that the other person is wearing, carrying, or sharing. They forget an important key. Did you catch it? They have NOT followed their natural, genuine curiosity. They believe that they have made an attempt to establish rapport, but in reality, they have just checked something off their "invisible list."

An example of some people's list of important to-dos to connect:

- ▸ Say, "Hello!"
- ▸ Ask question
- ▸ Get what I want
- ▸ Leave

Looking at the photo above, I noticed his haircut and how it goes up in the back. I was going to give you an example around his haircut but I noticed that I was not really curious about it. I was just trying to provide an example. Like checking it off my list. I noticed his hair and I'm not curious about it. Therefore, any question I would ask would fall flat. It would be fake. The un-realness could place more space between us rather than make us closer. Now, you might be a hairstylist or love to talk about hair, or just wonder how people choose to get their hair cut. Not me. Although I am often curious what compels people to color their hair. If you are curious, what could you ask that would bring you closer to connection?

I suggest that *not* following your natural, genuine curiosity more closely aligns with manipulation than connection. It is tricky for me to explain what manipulation is for you, because this "place inside where only you are the master" is different for each of us. The self-work in this book helps you understand this place inside yourself. One important way to learn about this "place" inside of you is to be clear about your intent, as we discussed in the previous chapter.

When your process of connecting with someone is mechanical, then the genuine curiosity that can create the connection is gone—as if just because you asked a question, you have fulfilled the requisite for establishing rapport. When a cook first learns to cook, they follow recipes, doing their best to do all the steps perfectly. It is mechanical, a process that lacks new inspiration. As cooks become chefs, they begin to change recipes, adding little bits of something new, curious to know how it will turn out. Here, you are the chef, and it's your job to add something new to the process each time. Your spice cabinet contains a big glass jar of natural, genuine curiosity. Your job is to add a pinch to the relationship from moment to moment. Perhaps some of the stories below will help you find the place where curiosity rules within you.

▶ Antidote: Develop deeper curiosity

Finding the spark within yourself to be curious about other people could be the most challenging piece for you. I believe that following your natural, genuine curiosity is a skill that we all have but may have forgotten. Watch children. They are naturally curious about the world and people and ask great questions until we

teach them not to. For instance, in her blog titled "The Teacher is Talking: Kids Say the Darndest Things," Leslie Lindsay quotes a four-year-old named Rio as having said: "If the day I came out of your belly is called my birthday, what is the day I went in called?"[26] Can you imagine Rio's parents dodging the question, or worse, making it unacceptable for him to even ask? We just need to remember what it is like not to suppress our natural, genuine curiosity. We need to unlearn the things that prevent us from being and expressing our natural curious selves. Instead, I encourage you to relearn what it requires of you to be your natural, genuine, and curious self.

Did you know?

We set out to research how many questions people ask each day. Our intention was to take the "global pulse" on curiosity. Sources ranged widely. But the common thread was that kids ask anywhere from 40,000 to 438,000 questions in the three years between the ages of two and five.[27] One study done in the UK found that from breakfast at 7:19 a.m. to tea time at 7:59 p.m., the average parent is faced with answering a question from their child every two minutes and thirty-six seconds.[28]

Data for adults presents a very different story. On average, adults ask six to twelve questions per day. Keeping at that pace, we'd have to live 3,333 years to catch up with the curiosity level of the average five-year-old!

Where does our curiosity go? Did we learn everything there is to know? Probably not, seeing as nine out of ten parents from the same study report that they have secretly used Google to answer their child's questions.

In the rest of this chapter, we share new tools to invite the benefits of curiosity back into your life, your home, your work, and your relationships.

Students will often ask, "What if I'm not curious about anything they are wearing?" If you are truly not curious and you cannot find that curious place within you, then DON'T ask. If there is something else that you are curious about, then follow that. Do they have something they are carrying or sharing (or even a hope, an aspiration, a pain) that you are curious about? Follow that curiosity.

Recently, I was meeting someone new, and I could not find anything he was wearing that I was curious about. However, he did have a small scar on his forehead. Even though asking about his scar in some way seemed taboo, I went ahead and asked—I discovered a great story from it and we began to build a relationship of trust. He knew that I wanted to be real and present with him.

I will offer a word of caution here: following your natural, genuine curiosity is a skill that needs to be developed (or re-learned). I have noticed that some have never lost it. However, most of us left curiosity behind as we grew older. If you are finding that you are not experiencing natural, genuine curiosity on a regular basis, check to see if you have a pulse. If you are dead, then stop reading this book; you have more important things to attend to. If you are alive, check to make sure that you are not part of the walking dead: those of us who have killed our awareness and are blind to the beauty around us. My guess is you are not part of the walking dead if you are reading this book because you are curious about how to ask better questions. (Or you may be really bored and this was the book sitting closest to you.)

Joking aside, if you are finding that you are not frequently curious, then maybe this is an opportunity to deeply explore what it is that inhibits your curiosity. Three questions that have helped me be more open to what is around me are:

▸ What is this moment teaching me?
▸ What is happening here that I am curious about?
▸ How does this person see the world from their perspective?

Let's look at the first question as an example: "What is this moment teaching me?" It seems like a simple question, but it's full of depth and can *never* be fully answered. The question invites you to be taught, to turn on your desire to be taught, and to be open to being taught. It invites those who are thirsty for knowledge to explore. Curiosity leaves me the moment I enter the space of "Oh, I got this figured out." My wife dislikes it when I have her figured out and loves it when I'm still curious about who she is and how she sees the world. Actually, when I have her "figured out," I no longer see her. I see who she was, not who she is or who she could be. When I'm curious, it takes us back to the time when we were falling in love. Full of discovery, exploring in a place of awe. Your curiosity gives a person the choice to be who they want to be, rather than what you want them or assume them to be!

Try it right now. Look around you. Pick anything or anyone. What is that thing or person teaching you? As I do this right now, the first three things I see are things that I made: a very unusual set of three-sided bookshelves that appear to be floating and wrap around a square brick chimney, a metal banister above a spiral staircase, and tiny wood shelves that I was inspired to create after seeing something similar at an art exhibition.

So, what is that teaching me? I like to be surrounded by things I made . . . no. When I really sit with the question of, "What is this moment teaching me?" I see that there is more to the story. I like to know where things come from . . . yes. Yet, there are other things in the room that I don't know the origin of. Their beauty is far greater than anything I could make, especially if they are made with glass and metal, two materials I have lots of experience working with. I love to be around things that are beautiful and handmade, with a preference for a story of where they came from. Deeper still is that I LOVE to know *how* things are made, so much so that I want to explore if I can make them, and if I have not learned to work with that material yet, I want to be surrounded with the potential to learn. I did not have this clarity until I asked myself the question, "What is this moment teaching me?" and stayed with answers long enough to write it down here just now.

Your turn. What is this moment teaching you? Ask this question from moment to moment and see what occurs for you. Do it especially when emotions are high. You may be surprised by the answers that show up. Then ask yourself the same question again and answer more deeply this time. Develop a habit of fierce, relentless curiosity and the world will reveal its secrets.

I am sometimes surprised by what stirs my curiosity. What seems to catch me off-guard the most is when I discover the way individuals view themselves in the world, or how they've come to settle on their belief system. The way people dress or what they carry around with them offers clues about how they see themselves. If you can ask a question around an "item," you might just find a belief that is buried that could be insightful for both of you.

While writing this, I reflected on what I carry. I asked myself, "What do I carry with me that would be a doorway into my beliefs and how I see the world?" The first and obvious answer is the small flashlight hanging on my computer bag. It seems I always have a flashlight within an arm's reach. There is one in each car, several in the house. Not really big flashlights, but small, "easy-to-carry-with-you" flashlights. I don't know anyone else who has so many small flashlights—unless all of us small flashlight users are hiding in the closet (that might be why we need a flashlight). I may use mine only once a month, if that, but when I need it, it's the perfect tool, and I'm thankful one is readily available. These flashlights, one of which is usually hanging from my bag, are a doorway into my world. I feel the need to be prepared for moments when times are tough and I find myself in the dark. During those instances, I will be ready to shine the light on the subject. EEK! As I type this, I am learning that this light might be a symbol of who I want to be in the world.

What do you carry that might be a reflection of who you are?

Here is part of my list:

- I am almost always wearing wool.
- I wear shoes built for long distance walking.
- My briefcase is a backpack so I can walk long distances.
- I almost always have one more layer of clothing on than I need.
- When it is sunny, I'm often wearing a hat with a bill but not a baseball hat.
- I carry a small rubber ball with me at all times—the super bouncy kind you get from gumball machines—and am always ready for immediate play.
- I have a multiplier tool with me most of the time.

Also notable are the things you won't see when we meet:

- a wallet
- a wedding ring (and my wife doesn't mind)
- bodily ornaments of any kind

This first list illustrates my desire to be outdoors and keep warm while exploring. What about the second list? I'm still trying to figure that out, but I think it most likely points to the fact that I like to keep things simple.

Look at the people close to you through a new lens and see what you discover. Maybe they are like my mom, whose purse is so big that you can ask for almost anything and she will fish out something that works (my flashlight seems small in comparison to her ability to clean, cut, or sew at a moment's notice). On the other hand, maybe the person you're observing sees themselves as a minimalist—like my wife, whose small blue purse has a red wallet and a yellow date book. She loves color! What do these purse preferences suggest? My guess would be that the minimalist is comfortable asking for what she needs when she is out in the world. Someone like my mom is either uncomfortable asking for help or enjoys being the one to provide for those who do ask. I should ask her about that!

Once you come up with a theory about how someone close to you is experiencing the world, ask for their thoughts on the topic. Follow your natural curiosity and enjoy a meaningful conversation. Then, try extending this exercise to strangers you encounter. See what happens.

A student once asked how to remain curious. She recognized that she used to be curious but felt she no longer was. In her case, it seemed to boil down to fear. Something scared the curiosity out of her. In response, I shared a thought that I learned from Marianne Williamson's Return to Love: *"There are only two emotions; Love and Fear. We can interpret fear as a call for love."*

Somewhere along the way, this student may have made so many choices out of fear that she forgot what it was like to make a choice out of love.

Choosing curiosity closely aligns with love. It is hard to be curious when making choices based in fear. Examine your own life and see what is true for you. When you brush your teeth, do you do it for love of self and good health? Or do you brush out of fear of your next dental appointment? What choices have you made today? Were those choices inspired by fear or love?

On the other hand, it's possible this student may be so well educated that she has learned the power of figuring things out. "Figuring it out," however, is different than being curious, being full of wonder. Traditional schooling has taught us to provide answers—the "right" answers—for which we all are rewarded. I'm suggesting that you ask questions to which there are no "right" answers and see what you learn. Become the teacher in the drama of your life, and learn what the characters tell you about the world. Curiosity and wonder are about being open to all kinds of possibilities.

Notice what happens in your mind when you look at the following word scramble puzzle.

What word can you spell by unscrambling the letters IAANTOOEOMOP?

Time is ticking.

Got it yet?

What is happening to your brain as you focus? What do you notice about your thoughts as you narrow in for a particular answer?

Compare that to this puzzle.

How many words can you make using only the following letters: IAANTOOEOMOP?

Now you are allowed to look for anything and see if it fits. Your thought process is closer to wonderment, although wonder is bigger yet. With wonderment, there is no one answer, but somehow it all connects in some grander scheme more closely resembling awe. Wonderment invites exploring the world around us without *knowing* all the right answers. Perhaps there are many answers instead of just one. What contributes to human happiness? How does a tree make a leaf? How does a loving family turn hateful in such a short period of time? How does the sky turn so many different shades of color so quickly at sunrise?

For those who just need to know, the anagram of IAANTOOEOMOP is . . . okay, clue first. A word of words—a word that can be used if you were talking about sizzle, buzz, zip . . . onomatopoeia. Now you can relax and wonder about the word's origin.

Ever noticed that the best way to kill a question is with an answer? When a juicy question has been asked and someone gives a definitive answer, the question dies. The puzzle is over. The wonderment is gone. Exploring is finished. The most obvious illustration of this point in modern times is the fact that people are more likely to pull out a cell phone and default to web browsing rather than allow conversational exploration to continue.

Did you know?

Neuroscientists have found that following our curiosity has powerful effects on the brain.

Matthias Gruber and Charan Ranganath, two neuroscientists at U.C. Davis, found that brain activity ramped up in regions that transmit the molecule dopamine, which regulates our pleasure and reward systems when we allow our curiosity to lead us.[31] "This anticipation is really important," says Matthias, "because the more curious a subject was, the more their brain engaged."

They also discovered that greater interest in a question would predict not only better memory for the answer but also better recall for other information such as a person's face.

Curious minds show increased activity in the hippocampus, which is involved in the creation of memories. In short, want to remember something or someone? Turn up your natural curiosity.

*If you'd like to follow your curiosity now, you can access more free resources and a behind-the-scenes video from us on this chapter at **www.weand.me/rapport**.*

▶ **Tool: Stay present**

An important key to making a connection is to be present in the moment. It is a sure cure to checking things off your invisible list. Ask yourself:

"What is this moment teaching me right NOW?"

Your only teacher can be found right now, in this moment. Sure, you can reflect on past moments, but learning only happens in the here and now. Our minds like to run to two places: the future and the past, both of which are entirely comprised of stories (that we made up) about what we think already happened (usually from one perspective) and what we think will happen. One way to escape these one-sided stories is to return to the reality happenings of the present. There is nothing more authentic than what is happening right now.

The importance of "being present" played out for me just before the beginning of a class where I had worked with students for several weeks.

A woman named Ping sat next to me in the circle as class began, settling in by placing her coat on the back of the chair. It took her a second to notice me sitting next to her. After a few moments, she looked up at me and said, "No offense. I am going to move over a few seats." She then moved her coat over to her new seat and sat back down.

What was I to do? How could I stay present? What would you do?

Staying present requires noticing the things that are

happening now. When you find something that someone is wearing, carrying, or sharing in order to create a connection, it is in the present. It is right there in front of you.

So, was I brave enough to be present? Ping was presenting something that triggered my curiosity. I wanted to know what that seat switching was about. I couldn't help but wonder about the choices she was making right now. So, I dove in to connect.

I responded with "None taken. What makes you want to move? I'm curious."

She said, "I'm afraid of you." After hearing herself, she quickly added, "Not just you, but all teachers."

I smiled. What do you say when one of your students says they are afraid of you, especially when you have worked hard to connect and have made a concerted attempt to remove all barriers that the teacher-student dynamic position can create? I could have let it go. I was certainly tempted to because class was about to begin and I was not sure I had time. Moreover, I was afraid it was too much, too fast at the start of class. But I knew that if I let it go, I would be adding to the circle of fear that existed for both us because I wasn't choosing to see all of her. This was not how I wanted my class to move forward, so I said, "What have I done to contribute to this fear? Help me understand."

This time she smiled and said, "Nothing. It is just who I am when it comes to teachers."

"Okay, Ping. What can we do to move toward connection rather than separateness? Would you rather be just a number in this class?" Still very curious about her choices.

She was quick to say, "No!" Then there was a long pause as she considered her options. "Well, I guess I could sit in that seat next to you?"

I smiled, patted the seat next to me, and said, "Thank you for sharing and naming your fear. I promise I will not bite!"

She smiled and then moved back to the seat next to me.

As she settled in with her coat for the third time, I said, "I will also promise to ask you for permission before I challenge you hard. Would that be okay, Ping?"

I wanted her to know that she still had choice.

She nodded.

"And know that my job is to see all of you and to push you to be the best you can be. Are you willing?"

I made my intent clear and still acknowledged her choice.

She responded with a big smile: "Yes, that is why I took this class, but old habits are hard to break."

"Yep, that is why you need the muscles of all these people to help you focus on the habits you want to break. Let's have fun working on what you want to work on. You have made a great step forward and class has not even started yet."

I wanted to acknowledge the choices she has made.

This moment was a turning point for her. She was able to be much more present in class and answer some tough questions she wasn't able to before. Prior to our exchange, she had been very reserved, but now she was a different person. She knew that I heard her and that I saw a piece of her that she was not sure she understood. She could now *leverage that knowledge and explore more deeply, simply because she named her fear, acknowledged it, and choose not to let it control her. Fear was now just a wise counsel that she could listen to but was no longer her dictator.*

Being present to what is, rather than what I would like it to be, was critical for me in seeing Ping. By being clear with my intent, I was able to be with her, and she could make her own choices without feeling pressed to do so.

It is important to note that there's something to be said for setting aside judgment and allowing ourselves to feel playful and delight in who people are. Even if they are radically different from you. Rather than judging, naming, and placing this person into a "box," find amusement in their place in the world. It's a skill anyone can cultivate. It is human nature to attach a label to things that are new to us and to fear what is new. Can we train ourselves to say, "Oh, well this is different—I wonder what this is about?" Transform fear into curiosity, and play with other perspectives. Even in the most serious of situations, the beauty comes from enjoying the process of discovery for the sake of discovery rather than trying to check a few things off our list. There's not a right answer, and it is important for us be okay with that.

After my successful encounter with Ping, I had another experience several weeks later that reminded me I still had (and still have) a lot to learn about being present.

Similar to Ping, a woman named Ling sat next to me, moved to another seat, and said, "Sorry, I don't like to sit next to the teacher." I smiled, and then my interaction

with Ping flashed in my head. Suddenly, a big part of
me was in the past. I jumped to the fear that was present
several weeks ago and expected it was the same now
in the present moment. I asked, "Ling, are you afraid
of me?" I could have done much better to be present to
her concerns right now, but because I was in the past,
I brought that past (and the feelings associated with it)
into the present moment. It totally flopped.

Ling's response was, "No!"

I said, "Really?" with a tone that made the question
mark huge.

Now she was in a place where she needed to defend
herself. She quickly replied, "I don't like to turn my head
so much to listen to the speaker. I assume you are going
to talk a lot so I would need to turn my head a lot." What
does one say to that? The best I could muster was, "Well,
actually, I won't be saying much today. I hope you will."
We were not closer. We were further apart. She did not
trust me to see her. She trusted me to project unfounded
feelings onto her. That was no way to build a connection.
I had lost the connection to the present moment.

Staying in the present can be difficult because the past and future
are such tempting places to go. They seem so much more predict-
able than the present—or so we tell ourselves. Nevertheless, the
power of connecting is in the present.

When you use the tool of observing what someone is wearing, carrying, or sharing, it is in the present. It is right there in
front of you. All you need to do is ask about it. There is no need

to bring in the past or even the future (unless they do that). Do whatever you can to stay in the present moment. If you ask, "How was your weekend?" then where did you suddenly go? Directly into the past.

If you want to connect quickly, identify something taking place at that very moment or turn your attention to something in the room. If the person you are trying to connect with has brought something into the room from their past, then it becomes part of the present because they are thinking about that object right then and there. It is an invitation to meet them. Join them there. For instance, if someone walks into the room chatting about last weekend, then meet them there if you think this topic peaks your curiosity.

On the other hand, if you take someone who is in the room into the past, you are taking them somewhere they currently are not. In this case, it will normally take longer to connect as there may be unconscious resistance, and they will need to decide if they are moving toward you. In addition, you will both need to navigate to the same location in the past. Although this can potentially establish rapport, it's a slow journey. If it works for you—great. It is a tool in your toolbox.

Remember, the tool is to find something the person is wearing, carrying, or sharing that you are naturally genuinely curious about and to ask an open-ended question. What makes it work? Think about what happens when you get up in the morning. You make choices about how the world is going to see you by selecting what to wear. Some accessories are important to you (e.g., a ring) or have a story attached to them ("I got this hat on a trip to New York City"). By asking someone a question about an item they are wearing or carrying, you are likely to strike a personal chord. You are connecting to a choice that they made as recently as that morning. If you are also following your own genuine curiosity, then it is highly possible that you will both be slightly vulnerable. They will be vulnerable in telling their story, and you will be vulnerable by asking and by deeply listening. That vulnerability begins to build a bridge of trust between the two of you.

Some of you may be wondering if this tactic is too personal. Yes, it is more personal than asking about the weather, sports, or general topics, but no, I don't believe it is too personal of an approach if you are making an earnest attempt to connect. After all, connecting with people is about getting personal. You are telling folks on a deep level that you are able to be real, and you are inviting them to do the same. Your intention and your actions line up.

Take into account that the other person has a choice. They can choose how to respond to your invitation.

At the start of a recent workshop, a participant strolled into the room wearing a New York Yankees hat. Based on his gait and the way his clothes hung, I guessed he was from the city. I introduced myself and asked, "Are you a fan?" and pointed to his ball cap. "Yep!" he replied curtly then sat down, pulled out his phone, and started typing away.

His response encouraged me to think about my approach. I realized that it failed for two reasons. First, I had asked a closed question, which encouraged a short reply. Second, I had no interest in sports. I was not following my own genuine curiosity. I did not care to know if the Yankees won or who was playing well. I was faking it. Moreover, he knew it, thus his phone was more interesting. I never found out if he was from the city or learned much about him at all. I failed in my attempt to build a rapport with him.

Lesson learned. Or so I thought, until several workshops later, another participant arrived wearing a Yankees ball cap.

It was the first thing that I noticed; he was a head taller than everyone else. The first ball cap encounter flashed through my mind, and I smiled as I thought, "Don't ask about the hat, silly." A funny thing happened: as he moved closer, I noticed that his coat, his backpack, his pants, and his shoes all had the team's logo on them. When he took off his jacket, he was wearing a Yankees jersey.

This was just too much, yet, I was telling myself, "Don't ask. You are not curious about sports. Don't ask." Looking back on this moment, I can see the fear of failure pulling me away, creating more distance between him and me. I was so caught up in the failure of the past rather than being present to NOW, that I almost skipped saying hello to him completely. Luckily, I paused and heard this voice in my head, "You're curious here! What are you curious about?" I responded to myself, "How did he become such a fanatic?" The voice in my head responded, "Then ask that!"

Still, I was slow to ask anything. I was nervous about failing again. Fanatic seemed like strong language and loaded with judgment. How could I soften it? And then I remembered that fan is short for fanatic—so I went for it.

"How is it that you became a Yankees fan?"

He told me an intriguing story about how his father took him to his first game when he was six years old, then mentioned his memories of his father at the game and that his father had since passed away. This story was so powerful I could see why he was such a fanatic. I almost wanted to become a fan, too. I then had to ask if he considered himself to be a fanatic, and the conversation flowed with ease.

Later, when it came time to ask him a tough question during the workshop, it was easy for me to ask and it was easy for him to respond. He knew that I had made an attempt to understand him and was willing to share more in order to continue building on that trust.

But what if everyone in a room is wearing the same thing, as is often the case in the business world, where wearing suits is a virtual requirement. You have to work harder to find unique elements, but if you look closely, you can typically find something. If there is a strong culture of uniform compliance, there is also often a little rebel inside many folks that encourages them to set themselves apart with a subtle accessory that says, "This is me." Find it and, if you are genuinely curious about it, see what happens when you ask about it. A rebellious touch can be quite revealing.

▶ Trap: Giving compliments

Another common trap that people fall into is giving compliments. There are several potential pitfalls in this approach. I ask people to look for something they are genuinely curious about, and they look for something they like. Somehow, they equate genuine curiosity with something requiring a compliment. I know this because I have witnessed many students open a conversation with statements such as, "I like your . . . purple hat," and then follow up with a question.

This is not an opportunity for you to judge fashion sense. Your job is to notice what you are curious about, to notice what choices the other person has made, and to ask about those choices. Sometimes people offer weak or insincere compliments in hopes of connecting, but others will always know when you're genuine and when you're faking it. So, if you genuinely love it, go ahead and extend the compliment. However, actively *looking* for something to compliment is not what we are talking about here.

On the flip side, I have seen people succeed in making a connection over something that wasn't necessarily to their taste but which made them curious nonetheless. Don't believe me? Try it out and see what happens. Is it possible for *you* to be curious about things that you do not like?

A compliment is a judging statement, which generally creates distance rather than closeness. Compliments are tricky because it's difficult to understand the intention behind them. For example, at times a compliment is used as a way to butter someone up before asking for something.

> When I worked as a cook at a bar, I always knew when the waitresses needed something special. First, their tone was all lovey-dovey. "Oh Willlllll." Then the compliment would come: "You're the best cook ever." I would smile and wonder what would come out of their mouths next. Inevitably, it was something like, "We got a live one out

here, and they don't care about cost. They want us to take
everything you would normally put in a burrito and make
a pizza with it. Like a Mexican meets an Italian. Can you
take care of that for me?"

Sound familiar? We tend to get a little guarded when someone pays us a compliment, especially when we know it's not true (I'm not the best cook ever, ask my wife). We assume they want something from us. When the waitresses were throwing compliments my way, I felt I braced myself for what was coming next, fully expecting a difficult request.

Another problem with paying a compliment is that the other person may feel compelled to return a compliment, which may or may not be genuine. "Thanks, I like your hat, too!" Nobody knows where he or she stands in such an exchange.

Finally, compliments can be used in a manipulative way. Some people give compliments in order to ingratiate themselves to others, or with the belief that flattery is a way to get what they want from the other person. The subtext of "I like your hat" could be: "You intimidate me, so I'm just going to compliment you rather than try to engage with you."

I once had a class in which I asked students to practice
using this curiosity with three strangers. This was their
self-work for the week. As the students shared what they'd
experienced over the course of the week, an interesting
learning moment arose. One student, Bob, went to a local
market and, as he was preparing to check out, he decided
that he would try to connect with the cashier for his

"self-work." As Bob was relaying his story, I could see he was visibly nervous. He broke out of his story, looked up at me, and said, "I don't understand why you asked us to do self-work with strangers, Will! It does not work!"

I smiled and asked him to tell us what happened. He said he'd noticed a tattoo that covered the cashier's entire chest. He saw this as an opportunity and said to her, "Nice tattoo! Where did you get it?"

Her response shocked him. In a cold voice she said, "I don't talk about it! Paper or plastic?"

I was about to ask Bob some questions to help him understand the trap that he'd unknowingly fallen into. Fortunately, I did not need to. As is often the case, the teacher was another student.

Steven chimed in and said, "Are you talking about the cashier at Conifer's Convenience?"

"Uh-huh," said Bob. He sounded unsure if he was excited about someone knowing who he was talking about.

Steven said, "I saw her, too, and I decided to ask her about her tattoo, too!"

This came as a surprise to the majority of the class, myself included, and some of us even laughed. "What are the chances . . . ?" I heard someone ask.

Steven continued: "I also wondered about the tattoo, but before I asked her, I thought about how hard it must be to have a tattoo like that when you are a cashier. Before I could come up with a good question, it was my turn and all I could muster was, 'You must get comments about your tattoo all the time!'

She responded with a laugh and said, 'Like you wouldn't believe! It is rare for people to see me; they just see the tattoo. It is a rare individual that can see past the tattoo and see me.'

The conversation continued as she bagged my groceries, and we talked about how people don't see each other and just expect things to happen for them."

Steven felt like he understood a little bit about how this cashier saw the world in just a few moments.

There were some obvious differences between Bob's and Steven's efforts, even though Steven could not form a perfect question.

- Steven found his genuine curiosity by wondering what it was like to live her life in that small store with such a tattoo.
- He found that curiosity by seeing the cashier as a person, knowing she had feelings much like his own. He accomplished this not by adding her to a "To-Do List" or turning her into a project.
- He did not give a compliment like "Nice tattoo" but went right for what mattered.

Though Steven did not ask the perfect question, the heart of what he was asking came across positively and affected their interaction. He offered his ears and received an unexpected outcome.

▶ Antidote: Prioritize rapport

Some people tell me that they don't have time to establish rapport or that it is difficult to prioritize. They often give compliments as a way of connecting and then rush to try to get to the heart of the matter (which is manipulation). If you desire to do deep and meaningful work, you must use the time you have with people efficiently and effectively; this will strengthen your relationships. If you invest your time in building a relationship of trust, you will save time and energy. People will want to engage. Recently I observed a striking situation where someone did not take the time or make any effort to connect with those she was going to work with, and it showed.

> *I was a participant at a diversity workshop in which the presenter never looked at or connected with any of the participants before she began. The workshop was scheduled to start at 10 a.m. People began to arrive at 9:45. When the participants arrived, they found seats and sat in silence. Meanwhile, the presenter sat behind the podium, punching keys on the computer (it seemed like she was checking her email). Rarely did she look up or acknowledge anyone in the room. We all followed her lead and began to do the same with our electronic devices. A room full of people, and no one was talking. The silence was all-consuming. Some of the folks who arrived closer to ten noticed the room was quiet and stepped out to double-check the room number and confirm they had the right room. At 10:01 the presenter looked up, noticed how many open seats there still*

were, and said, "Let's give them a few more minutes. We will start in five minutes," and then went back to punching keys.

How did that make the people in the room feel? Did they feel honored for being on time? Did they feel honored for being present at all? A magic moment was lost. She'd been given the opportunity to use her time effectively and connect with her audience. Instead, she chose to spend time with the computer.

I assumed she was going to ask some hard questions—diversity is not an easy topic for most. Later in the workshop, she did ask a few profound questions, but each question fell flat. No one in the audience responded, and silence filled the room. No one wanted to answer her questions out loud. No one was invested in the process or the relationship. It was as if we were watching TV with a broken remote and couldn't change the channel. She needed to answer her own questions in order to keep the dialogue moving forward. To get her message across, she had to work harder and use more and more material. It also took more time (the workshop went longer than planned) and was much less dynamic than if she would have invested in building a relationship of trust from the get-go. Many participants left the room uninspired. I heard folks loading up in the elevator sarcastically saying, "Well, it was not a complete waste of time. We get diversity points even if it sucked, right?" Things could have rolled out much differently.

Have you had similar experiences where you were invisible? People want to be seen. See them and watch what happens.

I recognized what was happening, because a few weeks before, I had done a similarly poor job of establishing rapport.

I was running a series of workshops on diversity. The audiences for each workshop were a similar population, but each four-hour workshop had different folks in it. When I got to the fourth workshop on day two, I thought I had the material down and knew how I was going to roll out the program, so I skipped all the rapport building steps. I just jumped in and started, even as the look on their faces was saying, "Who is this guy?"

The workshop went horribly. Each time I asked a powerful question, it fell flat. I would pose what I believed to be a compelling question and wait a long time for someone to respond. Each time, the response was superficial or an attempt to avoid the heart of the issue. No one wanted to engage with this presenter who did not engage with them. It was a long four hours and I could not get back to a good starting point once I had made this mistake.

As the day progressed, I couldn't figure out why the workshop went so poorly, so I defaulted to placing blame on the participants. I told myself, "They did not want to be here; they were so unmotivated." As the participants were leaving, one of them said, "Hey, thanks for trying anyway." The way he said it sliced to the heart of the issue like a scalpel.

For me, trying has an element of failure in it, and I

*knew that I had failed, not the participants, and at the
time I was unsure what I had done.*

*Like Yoda once said in Star Wars: "Do or do not.
There is no TRY."*

How Rapport Can Be Applied in Groups

If you are working with a group and you want the group to work
well together, take on the responsibility of reducing social risk
as much possible.

*Several days after my failed diversity workshop experience
and still carrying around a taste of failure, I attended
another workshop in which the presenter, Jack, truly saw
each person as he or she came into the room, taking the
time to engage with each of them in some way. Sometimes
he used body language (a smile, a nod, an inviting wave),
sometimes he said just a few words ("Welcome!" or "Glad
you're here" or "Make yourself comfy!"), but most of the time
he engaged with them in some more meaningful way. In
addition, for each person, his approach was different. Let's
see how Jack applied what we have been learning to groups.*

Here are some of the things I saw him say or do:

> ▸ *He introduced himself to each person: "Hello,
> I'm Jack."*

> ▸ *When a participant responded with their name,
> he would look into their eyes and say the name
> a couple of times like it was a new word for*

him. Sometimes, he would ask about the story of their name, or where it came from, or how their parents chose it. Once, he briefly talked about the responsibility of naming his own kids, and how he felt like these were the most important decisions he would ever make for someone else.

▸ *After asking their name, he would then ask about something they had with them that he was curious about. Then he would ask a follow-up question, such as where they got it.*

▸ *When someone else in the room responded to the exchange he was having with an incoming participant—usually with body language—he would ask them a question, prompting them to also engage in the conversation: "You have a question you want to ask her about her bag? Go ahead. The point of today is to get us to talk with each other." And they always would. After he got the two parties talking, he would "be distracted," usually by someone new coming into the room.*

▸ *Once, he even got a new arrival included into the conversation almost immediately, and it seemed effortless. He just said, "I'm Jack." She responded with her name, then he said, "These kind folks are talking about the best place to buy bags, you look like you might have something to say about that," and he gestured to her bag, and then moved over to talk with someone else who was coming in.*

"Oh, that was smooth," I thought. I was impressed by how he saw each of them, honored their choices (i.e., acknowledging the bag), and then invited them to talk with folks in the room. It appeared that each person knew they were seen by Jack and they all felt welcomed. I was also amazed at how he instigated so many little conversations and connections. It was not a quiet room of people pretending to ignore each other, as we have all experienced upon entering a room full of strangers. It sounded like a group of friends.

Looking around the room, it was evident that Jack had come early to set the room up so it would work for what he was trying to achieve. He had his materials spread out and easy to access, as he needed them. I later discovered that he had come an hour early to be sure he was set up and ready to engage people as they arrived early.

Jack's actions encouraged me to think about my own actions a few days before. I did not take the time to connect to everyone in the group. Truth be told, I did not connect with anyone at all. They had become objects, and I felt like I needed to get through the day rather than be present to what was happening in the moment. I started the group at full speed. I was doing all the right actions (or so I thought) but did not connect with a single person. Why would they take one of my questions seriously when I wasn't taking them seriously?

Jack supported the group in working well together by taking the social risk himself. He made it okay for people to start talking to him and, more importantly, to each other. Not one person stepped back out of the room to check to see if they got the right place, because he welcomed them as soon as he could. He was able to build on those connections through our time working together and continue to build rapport that existed in the room. He made sure that each participant was seen and knew it.

▶ Trap: Feeling the need to connect to each person

You might assume that you need to connect deeply with each person before starting the gathering. Although that might be an ideal goal to strive for, it's usually not possible when you have a large number of people arriving in a small time frame. If this ideal is causing you stress, it is not serving you or the group. (I have seen practiced leaders connect with up to twenty people when they arrive within a fifteen-minute window before the program starts. As you practice, you will find your own rhythm.)

▶ Antidote: "See" them and get them connected to each other

The goal here is to make each person feel like he or she has been "seen." Some small acknowledgment like "Hello," "Welcome," or "Glad you are here" goes a long way toward putting people at ease. Even smaller acknowledgments like a head nod or gesturing to an empty seat can be effective, particularly if they are arriving after you have started.

▶ Tool: Connect first!

As soon as you can, get people connected to each other. There are numerous ways to do this. I like how Peter Block, famous author and consultant, breaks it down: he calls it "Connection before Content." Get everyone in the room connected to each other before you give them content to wrestle with. Your job will be to develop a question that everyone can answer and that connects to the purpose of being together. It is useful if the question allows for vulnerability and authenticity to show up in people's answers.

Two questions I recently created, based on the groups I was working with, are:

- ▶ What compelled you to say "yes" to the invitation to be here, and what about that is important?
- ▶ What are you aiming to achieve at work, and what about that is important?

Next, write your question so everyone can see it. Invite everyone to form groups of three or four with people they know the least about and have them discuss their answers. With some groups, it is helpful to suggest they try to fully listen to other participants' answers, without trying to fix it, make it better, or prepare to give an answer that is better than what they just heard. Just listen. Give them ten or fifteen minutes to work together. Once time is up, give them a thirty-second warning. After thirty seconds, stop the discussion (they will likely want to keep going) and ask the room: What struck you about what you heard in your group?

Allow one person at a time to answer. Your job is not to fix it, but just listen or reflect upon what you are hearing. After a number of people have shared, you will notice that most people in the room feel connected, even to those they have not spoken with. They will be ready to do deep work and will be ready for powerful questions.

Another way to connect first is to use *We! Connect Cards*™, a pack of sixty questions we designed to create conversations that matter. Among the cards, you find activities like Question Swap, in which people trade and answer questions for fifteen minutes before the meeting. They can create a space where everyone is connected and ready to get to work. You can find them at www .weand.me in our online store. You might have noticed samples of the cards sprinkled throughout the book.

Summary of Rapport

▸ Connect first!
▸ Follow your natural, genuine curiosity and ask about it.
▸ Find something they are wearing, carrying, or sharing that you are curious about and ask open-ended questions about it.
▸ Avoid traps associated with finding commonalities, faking it, or giving insincere compliments.

Another way to summarize this chapter is with three simple words: **Notice**, **Wonder**, and **Inquire**.

Self-Work for Rapport

Are you ready for the challenge? When we begin this type of work, some people are excited for the adventure of discovering the unknown; others may feel as if there is a real emotional risk involved. There is indeed some risk. You are pushing on a palpable boundary that has been set by both you and society. It is easier for people to connect with silence (or play with their phones) than to connect with a stranger. There is an awkwardness that the first person to speak has to push aside their fear to make something new happen. It can be challenging to take emotional risks in order to connect with others and to bring mindfulness to the process.

Your self-work, if you choose to accept the challenge, is to establish rapport with three strangers in the next week. I know that your mother taught you not to talk to strangers, but in this case, it's okay. Obviously, do what you can to manage the risk but also challenge yourself. There are all kinds of places to practice: on the bus, while standing in line, with the cashier (look for more than the tattoos), with the waiter, with the toll ticket attendant, in an elevator (yes, that one is challenging and I have heard many successful stories). Only you know where the strangers are in your life. Talk to them and see what happens. Then share your experiences at www.askpowerfulquestions.com.

If you learn how to establish rapport with people with whom you have no agenda (e.g., strangers), then you will more likely and more effortlessly connect with the folks that you are working with. This is the point. Connecting quickly will allow you then to ask powerful questions seamlessly.

One more note here. With all this being said, I'm not suggesting that your current methods for establishing rapport are wrong. Actually, it is best if you understand the ways you establish rapport now so you can leverage that knowledge and build upon those skills to establish even greater rapport with those around you. The tools presented here will help you establish rapport quickly so you can connect with folks immediately and do more of your work in making the world a better place.

Wherever you go, go with all of your heart.

— Confucius —

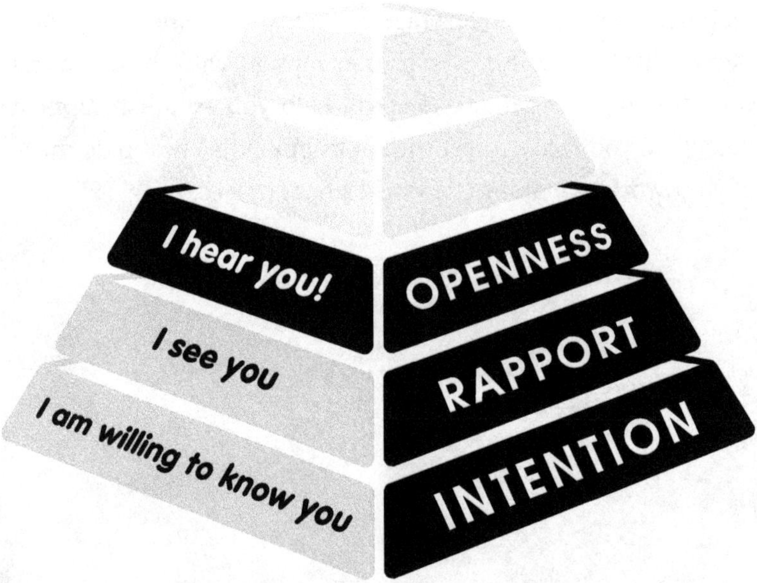
I hear you!
OPENNESS
I see you
RAPPORT
I am willing to know you
INTENTION

Chapter 3

Openness

You can tell whether a man is clever by his answers.
You can tell whether a man is wise by his questions.

— Naguib Mahfouz, Nobel Prize Winner[32] —

The Power of Being Open

Imagine that a group of friends chooses to go to dinner at a nice new restaurant. The hostess tells them it is going to be forty-five minutes before a table will be ready. They look at each other as their smiles fade, and one says, "What *should* we do?"

Just then, another set of smiling friends walks in, again being told it will be forty-five minutes before they can be seated. These friends look at each other and one of them asks, "What *could* we do?"

Which set of friends do you think created possibilities for themselves? The friends who asked, "What should we do?" or the ones who asked, "What could we do?"

The statements by each set of friends point to what is going on inside them. The first group, like in school, is looking for the "correct" answer. What is the "right" thing to do right now? The word *should* in their dialogue implies that there is an expectation for how the friends respond to this unexpected wait. The second set of friends took what was coming at them. Rather than problem-solving by looking for a correct answer, they created an evening of possibilities.

The second set of friends is already ordering appetizers at the bar, laughing, and having a good time. The first group is sitting on the bench with a look of resignation on their faces. What made the difference? Being open inside. How did that openness show up in the world? The "shoulds" were not in a place to see any other possibility. The "coulds" would allow for, or even create, other possibilities. By being observers, hearing should or could, we experience the difference in their language. No matter what we do on the outside (the words we say or the motions we make), we need to *be open* in order to ask a truly open question. I strongly believe, and have seen it often enough with my students, that if you are not open inside then you cannot ask a truly open question, no matter how good the mechanics of your question are.

For instance, you could ask, "What is your view on climate change?" That question would appear to be open. The topic is loaded. People will prepare to see a fight and expect to experience judgment. If you are not open to what will happen after the question is asked, then it is not an open question. If you are not available to all responses—*any* response—then you are not open. Believing so resolutely in absolute statements, such as "We should not have a plan to stop using fossil fuels because the market forces will take care of it" or "The only solution is wind power," that you cannot hear a different viewpoint indicates you are not open. If you are expecting a particular response rather than being "open to surprise," then you are not open.

A friend asks questions that I initially found to be effectively open but have now started to refer to as "the hook." Recently he asked me, "So, what do you think about the presidential campaigns?" Seems open enough, right? Yet, when I started sharing, he cut me off. "That's outrageous! Let me tell you . . ." and off he went for twenty-five minutes, barely stopping to catch a breath. I can summarize the twenty-five-minute speech for you in two words: "You're wrong!" No matter what I said to try to enter into the conversation, it was quickly dismissed because it did not fit into his worldview.

Maybe there's someone in your life like this, too. They ask you a thought-provoking question, and then even before you finish your answer, they have begun to tell you why you are wrong.

This dynamic can also occur when you both agree. Have you ever noticed that sometimes you stop listening when someone's ideas begin to sound just like yours?

What does it look like when you are being open? How about when you are not being open? Oh, that's where this conversation gets tricky.

Let's start by exploring this question: What is the opposite of open? I have intentionally used the phrase "not open" in the paragraphs above. Some would say the opposite of open is closed, and I partially agree with that. However, if I say the opposite of open is "closed," there is little I can do about it. Closed is a label that does not allow me to get inside and open things up. The door is closed, locked, and the key is thrown away.

What would allow me to open the door when I'm in this place where I'm not open? What would make me take notice and offer a key to opening up?

When it comes to connection, the opposite of open is the *need to be right*. A burning need. For some, it is more important than almost anything else, except for maybe the need to be loved or admired, and yet we all know people who have given up on love to satisfy the need to be right. If I'm feeling the need to be right, I'm closed to what you are saying, and I'm also not listening to what you are saying. I'm not open to who you are in the world or your desires.

For instance, if you asked, "What is your view on abortion?" and your own viewpoint is so resolute or absolute that you'll use any response as fodder to prove you are right, then you are not open.

When you ask questions for the sole purpose of proving to others why you're right, or when you try to push the conversation in a direction that supports your agenda, the other person will know (even if they don't verbalize that they do). They will sense that you are in the "prove" place and they will either prepare to prove you wrong ("Let the debate begin") or clam up (by literally going silent or replaying the same old tape). Replaying the tape, especially in the workplace, is often about spitting out the answer they think you want to hear—one that's worked in the past, or one they know will make you happy by playing to your ego or values. Asking powerful questions creates a new possibility—not a forced outcome—that creates something new. Letting go of your need to be right and being open to what is possible is a HUGE shift in creating new possibilities for yourself and those around you.

▶ Trap: Unknown triggers

The first step in opening up inside is being aware of what your triggers are, which cause you to no longer be open and limit your ability to listen. Your triggers are manifestations of your fears revealing themselves. If you look closely at a trigger, you can also find a fear vying for control. Understanding the fear allows you to react in a way you choose, rather than how the fear wants you to. A trigger is the activation of an emotional response. Once a trigger has been activated, the next action is often not a choice. It is a *re*action. We have a habit of reacting to the emotional response rather than making a choice about how to respond. A bit of a warning here—this is deep work. If it is a journey you choose to explore, you will have the ability to move the world in ways that you never before experienced.

For me, the things that drive my need to be right are still becoming clear to me, even after many years of exploring. One example is when I make a mistake, I need to justify to anyone who will listen, including myself, why I was actually right and that my actions fit the circumstances in that moment of time. Once I begin to have a handle on what moved me out of the open space, I can begin to take control and move back to being open. Are you aware of what moves you from openness?

What are your indicators that you are not listening and not being open to what is new? Do you have enough awareness of your moments in which you are not truly listening? Answer these questions honestly:

- What is it that I do when I have a *need* to be right?
- What is the story I'm telling myself when I have a need to be right?
- What is the story I'm telling myself when I am not really listening?

If you don't know the answers to these questions, ask those who you work and live with. They know.

When a colleague of mine asked us to identify what he does when he needs to be right, he was shocked that the group was able to tell him quite quickly that he exhales a long, loud breath and crosses his arms. Upon hearing this, he became quiet for a long time. He was unaware of this habit and was surprised that it was so obvious to others. He was now able to analyze those moments and identify his triggers.

Personally, my need to be right shows up anytime any of the following beliefs are threatened:

- ▸ I have made the right choice.
- ▸ I'm right.
- ▸ I'm better than those folks.

Once a trigger is activated, I can no longer listen. I don't even care what someone else has to say. My only desire is to either prove them wrong or leave.

Another colleague was stuck in a place for a long time because he had stories that he told himself with the following themes:

- ▸ I made a wrong choice.
- ▸ I did that poorly.
- ▸ Those folks are much better than me.

His responses centered around these thoughts and he had little forward action. Now that he's become aware of what triggers those responses in him, he is able to see the internal dialogue and make choices for how he wants to be in the world. When ideas show up that are different than his own worldview, he is able to be open.

Being open means being open to the unscripted, to the unknown.

Without knowing what our triggers are, we operate in the world in such a way that the fear is standing behind us, cloaked in invisibility, gripping our shoulders, and guiding us through life. We let the fear choose for us.

▶ Tool: Name your triggers

Identifying your triggers begins the process of revealing the fear. If you can name it out loud with a group of people who can listen, that is helpful. Ask yourself, "What is driving this reaction?" and write down the answer. You will start to see trends pointing to a fear that is ruling you. The fear is real and valid, yet it does not need to be the dictator of your kingdom. Acknowledging fear makes the invisible visible.

One extremely powerful way to move from the need to be right to being open is saying it out loud to the other person. For example, "Sorry, I just noticed that I was not *really* listening. I got hung up on a need to be right, and I know that is not helping us. Can you say that again? This time I am really going to listen to what you are trying to say. Thanks." A statement like that will change the conversation. The vulnerability expressed in this example is scary, and yet it is extremely useful in creating conversations that matter. You are naming your weakness and as you do, it shows up as strength. Authenticity in its truest form.

To ask open questions consistently, you have to be *open* and be ready to listen.

Data suggests that one of the most impactful ways to let go of our need to be right is to simply ask open-ended questions. Decades of marriage and family communication research has found that asking open-ended questions can validate people and make them feel heard—even when you disagree with what they are saying.[33] "I hear you" is the main message communicated when you are able to set aside judgment and ask questions with good intentions, natural curiosity, and a mindset of *openness* to however they might respond.

Beyond ensuring the people around you feel heard, asking open questions and *being open* to their response is an extremely tangible way to deploy Stephen Covey's timeless advice to "seek to understand before seeking to be understood."[34]

Open-Ended Questions

After you've clarified your intent and begun to practice establishing rapport and being open, your next challenge is to ask open-ended questions. Rapport is a great foundation for this. People will be willing to receive and think about your question if you have established a relationship of trust. The next step is forming questions that allow the other person to think in new and fresh ways.

Before we begin to explore open-ended questions, it is valuable to define what closed-ended questions are. What type of answers do closed-ended questions provide? A closed-ended question is not merely a question answered with the words "yes" or "no." Closed questions could also be answered by numbers, locations, or facts. Common closed questions include: "How old are you?" "How much did that cost?" "Where are you from?" "Where did you go on vacation?" "What color did you paint your house?" and even, "How are you?" Closed-ended questions have an expected answer.

Closed-ended questions often start with the words *Is, Do, Does, Where, When,* or *Who.* Notice how, when you start a question with one of those words, the other person generally gives you a short answer.

Which professions come to mind when you think of someone who uses closed-ended questions? Common responses are police officers, reporters, and trial lawyers. We often use closed-ended questions when we are trying to find quick facts or narrow a bunch of data.

There is nothing inherently wrong with asking closed-ended questions. There are times when using them is the best approach, like when someone has a strong emotional response to something you've said and you need to know if they are comfortable continuing the dialogue. The problem with closed-ended questions is that, in general, they are expected and will not elicit responses that are new, fresh, and powerful. We often are controlling the conversation when we use them. We are comfortable asking questions that are closed. That is a skill most of us have.

Now, let's look closely at open-ended questions.

Effective open-ended questions generate responses that are unrehearsed and unscripted, almost story-like in quality (they often are mini-stories), and the answers often invite more questions.

The key to asking open-ended questions is to be aware of what your questions start with. Open-ended questions generally start with *Why, What,* and *How.* In some cases, *Where* and *When* can also form open-ended questions, while closed-ended questions begin with *Is, Do, Does, Where, When,* or *Who.*

The Power of *How* and *What* and the Weakness of *Why* Questions

Recently, I found myself sitting in a fancy corner office, leading an energetic coaching session with an executive who had just shared that he'd said something to his boss and was now wondering if his words had been a mistake. I responded: "Why did you say that?" The conversation screeched to a halt as he looked at me with puzzlement, his forehead a mountain range of ridges.

Oops. I just made a mistake. Was it fixable? We had just been hitting a productive flow, but now it seemed like my client was getting defensive. He was about to exhale, lean back in his chair, and cross his arms (I had seen him do this before). "Wait just a moment, that was not a great question," I said; "Let me rephrase. What compelled you to say that to him?"

His response was a complete shift. He exhaled, placed his hands on the table, and said, "I feel like someone should share with him the fallacy of his thinking." Then he shared more. We were back in the flow.

How did one question cause him to nearly shut down? What happened with the next question that began to open him up again? Let's look at which trap I fell into.

▶ Trap: Asking Why questions thinking they are open

What is the question we ask most often when we believe we are asking an open-ended question?

Why?

While *Why* is considered an open-ended question, it does not elicit powerful and fresh answers. *Why* questions actually create defensive and scripted responses.

Think about times when someone asked you questions like these:

- ▸ Why were you late?
- ▸ Why did you do that?
- ▸ Why are you wearing that?

What did you feel like? Most often, people feel defensive. When you have been asked these kinds of questions, do you feel the need to defend why you are late, explain your reason for doing something, or justify your choice in clothes? Do you think about anything new or just give the responses you have already considered giving? (Did you notice the number of closed questions present here, including this one?)

If you ask someone why they were late, they already have an answer for you. They've been thinking about it the whole time they've known they were going to be late. If you ask a question that the other person needs to defend against, you are not going to achieve something new and fresh but rather prompt them to answer in a way that protects how they see themselves in the world. Notice in the following example how the need to defend can be so strong that we work hard to add things to our arsenal.

When I am rushing to get to an appointment that I'm late for, or my desire to protect an image of myself forces me to focus purely on defending my choices, I protect myself from the inevitable onslaught by mentally preparing my defense in advance. I was running late to work one time and still needed to stop to get supplies at a store on my way in. As I drove into the parking lot, I saw a man with an open car hood and jumper cables. I was excited—not to help him, but that his predicament provided me with an easy excuse for being late, and it would even make me look like a hero.

What does defensiveness look like? What do you do when you are feeling defensive? What do you notice about what those around you do when they are feeling defensive?

There is the obvious body language of defensiveness: crossing the arms over the chest and looking down, for instance. (Remember too, they could be cold, or their belly makes a convenient place to store their arms.) Really, think about it. What do you do when

you feel like you need to defend your point of view? Use your own body as a vehicle for learning. When I become defensive, I do one of two things. I will go very quiet, not say anything, avoid eye contact, and pull my shoulders forward (thus making myself appear smaller). Alternatively, I raise my voice, my face gets red, I make fierce eye contact, and I pull my shoulders back (and make myself appear bigger). Either way, I have disengaged from the conversation, mostly because I have a *need* to be right. As a result, I'm no longer interested in listening or being open. In the first scenario, I'm usually needing more time to get my thoughts gathered; in the second, I'm ready to pounce to prove I'm right.

How is your defensive dynamic similar or different?

We cannot be open and have a *need* to be right at the same time. You may have seen people make a fist, hide their hands (in their armpits or under their thighs when sitting), use their hands to do something else (fuss with a watch or other accessories, hold a drink with two hands), or turn their shoulders so they are no longer "square" to you.

When you observe these defensive postures, a question to ask yourself is, "How did I contribute to this?" You may have asked a question or made some kind of statement that is loaded with judgment. Sometimes it is obvious, such as when you ask, "Why did you do that?" In the workplace, especially when you're the leader, the receiver of that question knows that they are being judged for doing something "wrong." Although this question is sometimes not a judgment but genuine curiosity, the other person may still hear it as judgment. We will explore this as we go through more of the traps in the chapter.

▶ Antidote: Drop the Why from your questions

If you find that people are responding to your questions with defensiveness or non-engagement, they may be reacting to your judgment. Although it is true that you can ask questions full of judgment that create defensiveness, that do not begin with "why"—especially when using a certain tone—a good place to begin the process of asking powerful questions is to drop the *Why* in your questions and see how people respond. Examine the following tool to replace the *Why* in your questions.

▶ Tool: Powerful questions begin with How and What

Dropping the *Why* in our questions requires us to use something different to fill the void. Use *How* and *What* instead. Chances are, the heart of your *Why* question has some good material in it. So, drop the *Why*; use a *How* or *What* instead, and then do whatever is required to make the question make sense.

For example:

"Why . . . ?" becomes "What . . . ?"
"Why did you go to the market when you had what we needed?" becomes "What compelled you to go to the market?"

"Why are you wearing that?" becomes "What do you like about wearing that hat?" or "What is appealing about wearing that hat?"

"Why were you late?" becomes "What happened?" or "What happened that made it difficult to get to work?"

"Why . . . ?" becomes "How . . . ?"

"Why did you do this?" becomes "How did this happen?"

"Why do you charge so much?" becomes "How was this pricing structure decided?"

"Why do you think like that?" becomes "How is it that you learned that?" or "How did you come to that understanding?"

You will notice that in the examples above, the words in the original sentence changed in order to make the question clear. You will do this naturally as you try to find ways not to sound judgmental. When you create questions for which people will not feel the need to defend themselves, you will notice something else happening to your questions. The word "you" will show up less. The word "you" in a sentence may be perceived as a direct attack on the person (or persons) you are talking to, rather than what you are talking about. "Are we talking about 'me' or this thing around me?" Your posed question might be about something that they have done, but that is different than who they are. Remind yourself when asking a question that your intention is to critique the situation or the behavior rather than the person themselves.

One of my early teachers once said, "I love each and every one of you. The core of who you are is completely loveable, good, and pure. That does not mean that I may always like your behavior, actions, choices, or sense of humor." In a moment, she was able to separate who we were from what we were doing. As a result, she was able to give clear discipline that did not attack our self-worth.

If you can begin to make conscious choices around using "you," you will notice questions that are more powerful in your life.

For instance, let's look at a question in three iterations:

First, "Why did you complete that so fast?"

This question is filled with judgment and the person will need to defend themselves, proving both the outcome and the process of how they got there.

Second, compare the first question to "How did you complete that so fast?"

Here the question is being asked with curiosity, about an observation you've made. The person can answer by simply explaining what they did (maybe they developed a shortcut!). They still may need to defend, depending on your rapport, because the presence of the word "you" might confuse and lead them to believe that they are being attacked.

Third, compare the second question to "How was that completed so fast?"

Now the question is about the process and not about the person. There is less to personally defend against. There is much more to talk about now, and the focus can be on the process and how it was different than before. This will happen naturally, as you drop the *Why* and attempt to create less defensiveness. I suggest not focusing on the "you" component at first. That is a lot to think about. First, work on dropping the *Why*. That is enough of a mind workout to start with.

Dropping the *Why* from our questions requires us to think differently. We need to translate our *Why* questions into *How* or *What* questions. If your mind is anything like mine, this will give your brain a real workout. It is not easy because we have many years of practice in *Whys*, but the payoff is great. It is worth your time and effort. However, if you don't believe me, go practice and see for yourself.

What is your greatest struggle right now?

What is a time you learned something from a failure?

Did you know?

People who ask follow-up questions are also seen as more likable and caring. Personality psychologists even have a name for people who are adept at asking genuine follow-up questions that tend to invite more insight from their conversation partners. They call them "openers."[35]

Across three studies of hundreds of live one-on-one conversations, five researchers at Harvard identified a "robust and consistent relationship between question-asking and liking: people who ask more questions, particularly follow-up questions, are better liked by their conversation partners."[36]

This is significant because our intrinsic desire to be liked by others also influences our willingness to include and accept others.[37] We can actually promote *inclusion* and belonging in our organizations and teams if we simply promote more thoughtful, open question-asking.

It never hurts to have a few Harvard social scientists remind us of the age-old wisdom that it is more important to be interested than interesting.

▶ **Trap: Not being open inside while asking How and What**

One thing that gets in the way of asking good *How* and *What* questions is when we neglect to be open inside. An example that demonstrates "being open inside" is this: You are at work and a big problem is being discussed. You ask, "How did we get here?" Again, it appears as if the question is open, and it is better than, "Why did you do this?" However, it's not open if you are thinking:

- ▸ Who is to blame?
- ▸ Who is wrong?
- ▸ Jake needs to admit he made a mistake.
- ▸ Your view is the best.

For many who take on the task of dropping the *Why*, the need to be right is still very much present. They learn to drop the *Why*, but their questions are still loaded with judgment, creating defensiveness. When I have explored this challenge together with my clients, they notice that they are not open-minded about the content being discussed and they are trying to prove something. Alternatively, they are judging others in their heads: "I can't believe they are saying that! They are so wrong!" They have forgotten the needs of the other. Focus on connection.

▶ Trap: "But I already said why"

Your first awareness might begin with how often you ask *Why*. It is common for people to feel overwhelmed after they notice how often they use *Why* questions, and so they give up on this tool. No worries; this frustration is a normal part of changing your habits.

Using *How* and *What* in your questions is like learning a new language: it takes practice to develop the pathways in your brain that will make the *How* and *What* questions easier. When I was first learning Nepali, a thought would arrive in English, and I would translate that to a simple sentence in my brain before then translating the thought into Nepali, using the words I was learning and checking to see if the words made sense. Sometimes they did and sometimes they did not. Like a muscle that needs to be built, you need to exercise the language center of your brain in order to make *How* and *Why* questions habitual. My experience has been that those who have learned to speak a foreign language find this transition to *How* and *What* questions easier, because they have developed an awareness of how their brain works in formulating new sentences.

To drop the *Why* questions, a willingness is required—a willingness to practice and change how our mind works. This begins to build new pathways to form better questions (when you learn something new or change a habit, your brain *physically* changes itself to accommodate that newness). When you begin to practice this skill, you will find that your *Why* questions will flow almost automatically. Observe them. Before they come out of your mouth, catch them and drop the *Why*. Pick *How* or *What*. Add it to the beginning of the questions. Then move words or add words so the sentences flow as they should.

Some feel that once they've asked a *Why* question, it is too late to make an adjustment. I disagree. If you have noticed that you just used a *Why* question, that is your awareness growing. This is the first big push forward. Sure, you said it and you cannot take that back, but what you can do is use this as a moment of practice and fix it. (Oh, by the way, check your tone, too. Were you being judgmental? No amount of sentence changing will fix that. Check it.)

▶ Tool: Ask it again with How and What

Say something like, "Wait! Let me rephrase that question." (Optionally add "I'm working on asking better questions" if you want to be clear about your intention.) Then, rephrase your question. Of course, it will not be as good as if you catch it before it flies, but this will shorten the time it takes for you to create new questions and will be useful in the long run. It will also develop the pathways in your brain to ask more powerful questions faster and easier. (You don't want to develop pathways of "That was stupid" or "I wish I would have said . . .") The majority of the time, the receiver will let go of the first question quickly and answer your new question. Really. It will also help the receiver of the question to think in new and fresh ways. Go explore with it and see what happens.

Dropping *Why* from your questions is hard, and the word still regularly appears in my own conversations, unplanned. It is amazing how often we are unaware; even after learning about the value of *How* and *What* questions, we don't catch ourselves asking *Why* questions.

When I first began this work, and I was thinking I was doing a good job, I was shocked at how much I asked Why questions. Once I had awareness of how I was contributing to the conversation, I was unhappy with the results.

There are still times when asking *Why* might be useful, but using *How* and *What* more often and more regularly will be much more powerful, create less defensiveness, and allow the other person to contemplate the situation anew.

It is useful to have someone help you keep track. Asking others to point out when *Why* shows up in your exchanges can be turned into a fun game. Rather than being hard on each other, we can all laugh together about how the *Why* just snuck its way into the room, without being invited. Many of us have been using *Why* for so long we don't notice when it shows up. The support of others can bring your awareness into sharper focus.

▶ **Trap: Using "How come . . . ?" and "What made you . . . ?"**
It is common that when people drop *Why* questions, they will replace it with two other questions that are not powerful. When I work with people deeply in this material, I wait to introduce this next trap till they have a chance to practice dropping *Why* on their own. I have found that it is too much to introduce this next trap without some practice of dropping the *Why* questions. It is as if it short-circuits the system somehow. So, if you can manage, put the book down and practice some. If you need to keep reading before you get a chance to practice, then you have been warned.

Now that you have had a chance to practice, I will let you in on a little secret. You might have noticed two questions that you have started leaning on when you drop the "Why."

- ▶ How come . . . ?
- ▶ What made you . . . ?

Can you see that these questions create the same dynamic as *Why* questions? Yes, they start with *How* or *What*, but both of these questions are really *Why* questions in disguise.

▶ **Tool: Drop the "How come . . . ?" and "What made you . . . ?"**
Yep. Drop the "How come . . . ?" and "What made you . . . ?" questions too. You will notice that your questions will get even better. These questions often tempt you to place the "you" in your questions, resulting in people needing to personally defend against something, as we discussed in **Tool: Powerful questions begin with *What* and *How*.**

If you notice that you have been using "How come . . . ?" or "What made you . . . ?" it might be an indicator that you are not being open-minded. If you hear these questions come out of your mouth, check to see if you are open to surprise, open to an outcome that would be unexpected, open to an idea that you have not heard before. Ask yourself:

- Are you asking those around you to justify their choices?
- Do you want them to take a stance of defense?

If you answer yes, then chances are you are not being open. When I answer *yes* to either of these questions, I'm not open and I'm not doing a great job of listening, either.

▶ Trap: How does that make you feel?

One result of creating conversations that matter is that a fuller picture of the people involved develops. You will notice how feelings have an impact on those around you and you might be tempted to explore those feelings. When you start dropping *Why*, you may fall into a trap of asking, "How does that make you feel?" questions, thinking that you are doing a good job. Generally, this question has limited success as well. Let's explore that.

"How does that make you feel?" This is a common question, and some would argue it is even powerful. That is the reason it is used so much. When people practice asking powerful questions, some will go through a cycle where they fall back on this question frequently. People will notice your heavy use of this question and may try to find ways to skirt around answering it. When you begin to expand your toolbox of questions, you will notice that "How they feel" will show up in their responses more and more without the need for you to specifically ask, "How are you feeling?" (see Chapter 5 on Empathy). You can then reflect those feelings back to them (see Chapter 4 on Listening) and help them expand their own understanding of their feelings without ever asking, "How does that make you feel?"

This question does have a place in your toolbox, but should not be the primary tool to use each time you see an opportunity. To a hammer, everything is a nail. To this question, everything is a feeling (and little else), and that feeling must be discussed now (which might turn some people off). Although you might be ready to talk about their feelings, some people will be more willing to talk about feelings naturally in conversation rather than feeling as if they are at a therapy session. When you learn to listen with your eyes by keying in on body language, you will be better prepared to bring feelings into the conversation in multiple ways, rather than asking, "How does that make you feel?"

▶ **Tool: Use feeling- and thinking-based questions**

When we get to the chapter on Empathy, we will explore listening with your eyes and holding a mirror, so people can decide how to navigate their feelings. Until then, try rephrasing "How does that make you feel?" into feeling-based questions like:

- What feelings are associated with that experience?
- What did that feel like?
- How did your feelings get in the way?

Some people operate from a place of feelings and others tend to filter their lives though their thoughts. Asking, "How do you feel?" or any question rooted in feelings will exclude the thinkers. Try thinking-based questions like:

- What do you think about that?
- What are your thoughts about this?
- What are some of your thoughts about how that came to be?
- What thoughts are dictating your choices?
- How did your thoughts get in the way?

Even better than asking just a feelings-based question or just a thinking-based question is to ask questions that allow someone to respond as a "feeler" or as a "thinker," as it suits him or her.

Thinking- **and** feeling-based questions:

- So how are you taking the news?
- How are you adjusting to the news?
- How did you react when you heard that?
- What stood out to you?
- What resonated with you about . . . ?
- What struck you?

These questions allow someone to respond in a variety of ways. Some answers may be thinking-based rather than feeling-based. This might catch you off guard if you were expecting an answer loaded with feelings. Know that this is okay since a fair number of people like to "think things through" rather than "feel their way" through their lives. Therefore, these questions allow for people to respond in a way that is more natural for them. It is especially useful to employ these questions when addressing a group, allowing someone to respond with either thoughts or feelings.

Now that we have explored *How* and *What*, some of you might be wondering about the other question words: *When*, *Where*, and *Who*. Normally they are used in a way that is closed; however, they *can be* powerful questions. Let's explore that briefly.

When, Where, and Who Questions

When, *Where*, and *Who* questions may be considered open or closed. When the answers to these questions are a specific time, location, or person, they are closed. For example:

- ▸ When did you go to the hospital?
- ▸ Where were you born?
- ▸ Who are your parents?

However, in rare cases, and with skill, *When*, *Where*, and *Who* questions can be very powerful, open questions—like when the questions are asked in such a way that the answer does not fit a specific time, location, or is attached to a particular person.

For example, questions related to feelings:

- ▸ Where does that feeling come from?
- ▸ When do feelings like that come up for you?
- ▸ Who (or What type of person) makes you feel like that?

How about these examples:

- Where did you learn that truth?
- When did you begin to believe that was true?
- Who taught you right and wrong?

In the workplace, they might sound like this:

- When did we begin to notice this dynamic with our staff?
- Where could we find solutions?
- Who have we not included that could contribute in a meaningful way?

Though each of these examples *could* have a short answer, when you have good rapport with the other person, these questions will lead to more meaningful places in the conversation. Using *When*, *Where*, and *Who* as a starter to open-ended questions is a difficult skill to master. If you need to pick between dropping *Why* questions and using these types of questions, I would suggest starting with eliminating the *Why*s. This tactic develops your skills rapidly, garnering results more readily, and you can practice it more often. Once you are on the path to consistently asking *How* and *What* questions, then open your practice to include *When*, *Where*, and *Who*. These moments will be rare but useful in your conversation.

▶ Tool: Tell me . . .

There is one statement that functions like a powerful question and can work wonders if you are being open. It is not a *How* or *What*. It is not a *When*, *Where*, or *Who*. It is a *Tell me*.

"Tell me about . . ."

It is more of a directive. However, if you can say "Tell me . . ." from

- a place of curiosity,
- when your intention is about rapport and connection,
- and you are being open,

then something magical can happen. With its simplicity, it can be as powerful as a question.

Also, when someone has shared something that stirs your curiosity, it can be incredibly powerful to say, "Tell me more." This simple phrase informs them that you want to hear more, that you are curious about something they just said, that you want to *see* them. Often, they are happy to share more.

▶ Trap: Creating hypothetical questions

Early in my facilitation career, I wanted my questions to get to the heart of what mattered, but I wasn't always successful. I started leaning on creating questions that started with "What if . . ." The answers would often be surprising or insightful (or so I thought). One of my mentors kindly pointed out that these hypothetical questions are great if you want to learn about a "dream world" rather than the real world. I was not sure what she meant until the following week when I was interviewing someone new to be part of our team.

I said, "Imagine you are leading an expedition in a cave. You hear a loud crack. A student is down and holding his leg. What do you do?" I thought it was a great question and had great success with it in the past (or so I thought). I saw a look come over their face that resembled the faraway expression that takes over a child's face when they're playing make-believe. I had invited this person, who had never been in a cave, to play a game of make-believe with me, ultimately encouraging them to create an ending they thought I wanted to hear. If I learned anything from their response, it was that they are good at playing make-believe.

Later, one of the people I hired left the scene of a crisis. They could not handle it. The dreamer in them could play, when they were answering a question in a safe room. When the moment arrived for them to step up, they stepped down.

▶ Tool: Explore truth

Rather than using hypothetical questions to explore, use questions that open to someplace real. A place based on truth. This can require some fast thinking if you're already in the habit of asking hypothetical questions. Return to your intention. In the above hiring story, my intention was to explore how the candidate reacted when faced with stressful leadership situations in which there is no clear-cut answer. When your intention is clear, it is easier to create a question that will strike home. What questions might have been more effective?

Here are some possibilities:

- Tell me about a time when you had to deal with a stressful situation in which there were no clear answers and you took the lead.
- How do you deal with stressful situations when you are leading?
- What does your leadership look like when you are stressed and there are no "correct" choices?

Finding what is real (rather than make-believe) will also be valuable in other conversations outside of interviews. It is true that sometimes a hypothetical question can be useful when you want to open a new space and see what is possible. However, often the place it leads you does not give you firm enough ground to build from. In a hypothetical world, people can change the rules or the meaning behind what they said ("I did not mean it that way"). If you are about to ask a question that has a "What if . . ." style to it (even if you don't say those words), pause, check your intention, and see if you can ask it in such a way that gets to something real. Explore the truth.

In a dialogue around race, a white woman said, "I think interracial dating is wrong!"

I was tempted to ask, "What would your parents say if you brought home a Mexican man for them to meet?" Totally hypothetical. Not only would I be asking her to fit into a role that disagrees with her view, but I'd be asking her to guess what her parents' reaction would be. We would be creating a world of make-believe. I have found that I have better luck asking, "How have your parents influenced this idea?" or "How have you come to have this understanding?" or "What have you experienced that tells you interracial dating is wrong?" This might encourage her to begin telling stories, and yet these stories are backed on actual experience rather than imagining how the world might occur. We are getting someplace real, based on truth. Their truth.

Did you know?

Once, during one of our interactive keynotes, Will misspoke the subtitle of the book and said, "conversations that create matter." We both loved the mix-up because we have seen the power that questions have to spark action, *open* possibilities, and create material change within people and organizations.

Here are three wild, researched examples of the ability of questions to open our brains to new behavior and possibility:[38]

1. A study conducted with more than 40,000 participants revealed that simply asking someone if they were going to purchase a new car within six months increased their purchase rates by 35 percent.

2. According to the *Journal of Applied Psychology*, asking citizens whether they're going to vote in an upcoming election increases the likelihood that they will by 25 percent.

3. And in yet another study, researchers found that asking about one's intention to give blood raised donation rates by a modest but noteworthy 8.6 percent.

Questions cue the brain to contemplate a behavior. Decades of research has shown that the more the brain contemplates a behavior, the more likely it is that we will engage in it.

*If you want more concrete tips on how to ask great questions, you can access free resources and a behind-the-scenes video from us on the power of openness at **www.weand.me/openness**.*

From Interrogator to Conversationalist

Let's take a look at how changing the questions you ask can transform a conversation. If you ask lots of closed-ended questions, the experience will feel more like an interrogation, while using open-ended questions creates a more conversational experience.

Imagine that your teenage child is going to take your car out on a Friday night, and you ask:

- When will you be home?
- Where are you going?
- Who are you going to see?

You might have even asked similar questions of an employee at work:

- When will you be back?
- Where are you going?
- Who are you going to meet?

These questions will sound like an interrogation to your child or employee, and they invite short responses. The other person will feel the need to defend their thoughts and their actions. They will also try to figure out what you are "searching for." Your teenager may say the minimum required to answer your questions and receive the keys from you (or get you to leave so you will stop asking questions). However, you can take some time to connect with them and establish rapport (this skill needs to be continually practiced). You might have more luck getting complete thoughts by asking:

- So it's Friday; what do you hope to do tonight?
- What are you excited about?
- What concerns do you have?
- How will the people coming with you affect your evening?

Or with an employee:

- How will you use your time?
- What are some possible outcomes of your meeting?
- How will the people you will be meeting affect the outcomes?

Dropping the *Why* from your questions and instead using *How* and *What* will move you from a place of interrogation to a place of conversation. With your questions framed by *How* and *What*, you will find that people will want to share stories and give fuller answers. We tend to utilize closed-ended questions when we want facts.

Notice the difference between "When will you return?" and "How will you use your time?" If you only need to know what time they will return, then the first question is perfect. Consider the second question; will this get you what you want? More often than not, it will give you more than what you expected. It will give you connection!

Another subtle way that your questions can feel like an interrogation is when they're based on the negative. In other words, when your questions are based on what is wrong, what is lacking, or what is broken. When your questions are based on the negative, it's easy for the recipient to take your questions personally. If your question needs to focus on a problem, then make it clear that you are asking about the problem and not the person. Often it will be advantageous for everyone involved if you can take the core of your question and ask it in the positive.

There are simple ways that your choice of words unintentionally contributes to negative feelings. Even the words "problem" and "issue" are looking at what is wrong, compared to "topic," "theme," or "talking point." Noticing the language you use and how it contributes to the dynamic is powerful because you can control it. If someone is speaking and you cut them with "But . . ." or "Yeah, but . . ." you have already told them that they are wrong and you don't really care what they are saying. You might as well place them in a dark room, shine a bright light in their eyes, and ask, "Where were you last Saturday night?" If you have an underlying assumption that they are wrong, or that they are the problem, then you are not being open, and no matter what you say, they will understand that you think they are wrong. If, on the other hand, you can shift your mindset to a place of mystery, as an explorer embracing the unknown, real powerful questions (and connections) will be more commonplace for you. (See Self-Work for Openness for a way to practice.)

How Openness Can Be Applied in Groups

Most people find that asking a group of people open-ended questions is scary. People are afraid they will not be able to control the conversation or that it might travel down a path that is unpredictable. It is true that when you open a dialogue exploring the mystery of another human being, it is exciting and its very nature invites surprise. If you want simple, basic, or quick answers to your questions, then closed-ended questions might be the best solution. However, if you want to explore something new, bring new data to the surface, or learn the full truth, then opening up is the way to go.

In a group setting, it is useful to take a solo moment to make sure you're clear about your intention and open to unexpected outcomes. When you start the group, share your intention honestly and concisely. Take the risk to be real, acknowledge you don't have all the answers, and invite others to go on a journey with you, emphasizing that you can create something together that would not be possible to do alone.

The greatest value in being open and asking open-ended questions in a group is that everyone is now engaged in a way that was not possible before. If your question is a good one and people are connecting, everyone can choose to think, feel, and allow the new answers in the room to influence their thought process. Together, everyone creates something new.

Summary of Openness

Open Mindset

Having an open mindset requires you to be open to surprise and willing to explore the unknown around you. If you find yourself knowing how people are going to respond, or if you find that you are seeking an answer to support your own view, then you are not being open to those receiving your questions. A lack of openness creates a dynamic where people become cautious about sharing and maybe only give you what they think you are looking for. The need to be right might be so strong that it makes it impossible to be open to what is.

Open-Ended Questions

	Closed-Ended Questions	Open-Ended Questions
Begin With	Do Does Is Where/When/Who (generally closed) And various others	(What) (How) (Why) (may be attack, defense, judgment, accusatory) Where/When/Who (used in rare cases)
Answers Look Like	Yes/No One word I don't know Maybe/Sure Location, Fact, or Number	Unscripted Story-like Invite more questions
Others' Perspectives	Talk at you	Talk with you
Feelings	Interview/Interrogation	Sharing
Style	Interrogator	Conversationalist

Open-ended questions allow people to connect and build relationships. They allow people to respond in a way that is most fitting for them. These questions give them a choice about how to engage. If you honor that choice with listening and following up with more open-ended questions and reflective listening (see Chapter 4 on Listening), you will move toward connection and build relationships of trust.

The tool is to drop the *Why* from your questions and ask *How* and *What* instead. Make sure you do not fall into the "How do you feel" trap and don't beat yourself up if a *Why* question falls out. Just pick it up, rephrase it, and give it again. It will be okay. Really, it will.

Self-Work for Openness

Open Mindset

Learn your triggers. Ask those around you to help you name the moments that you become no longer open as suggested in **Trap: Unknown triggers**.

If that's not possible, there is a way for you to open the door of self-understanding. Find someone in your life (anyone, really—even a complete stranger), and find a topic about which you have opposing views. Engage in dialogue. Notice what happens as you engage in conversation—especially in the moments when you no longer are open to surprise or open to learning. Answer the following questions for yourself:

- What happens when you are trying to prove that you are right?
- What happens when you notice that you are just going to let the other person "have their way"?

If you look closely, you might see some of your triggers buried in the dialogue. One place that your triggers are hiding is where you are using the word "but" in your language. "But" points at a limited view you have of the world or a trigger that you have not come to terms with. The word "but" negates whatever comes before it.

Take, for example, "I love you, but it drives me crazy when you . . ." Are they going to feel the love? Or consider this example: "What you did here was great, but this part is going to cause a problem." What is the receiver going to hear? They are only going to hear the problem and not the great work they did.

This is true as well when you use "but" as a way of starting a sentence. If Ruby says, "We work in a trusting environment," and your response is "But all the office supplies are under lock and key," you are clearly saying that you don't believe in her view. The "but" or "Yes, but" at the front a sentence or a clause makes whatever they just said null and void.

Your next challenge: For a week, eliminate the word "but" from your vocabulary. You will find that you need a word to fill the void as you learn to speak in this new way. When the word "but" shows up, use the word "and." It will work most of the time: "I love you, ~~but~~ and you drive me crazy," or "What you did here was great, ~~but~~ and this part is going to cause a problem." As you eliminate the "but," look to see what limiting beliefs and triggers it reveals for you.

Open-Ended Questions

Your self-work for open-ended questions is to establish rapport with three more strangers, find something that you are naturally curious about, and ask an open-ended question (dropping the *Why*). Listen. Notice how the other person responds. Find your genuine curiosity and ask another open-ended question based on what they have said. Are their answers similar to answers you've gotten in the past, or did you hear new things in these conversations? Notice where the conversation goes and enjoy the ride.

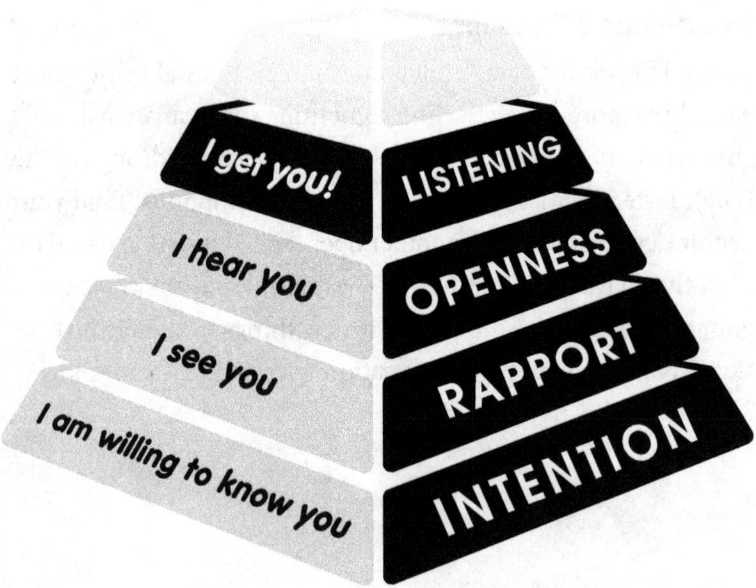
I get you!
LISTENING
I hear you
OPENNESS
I see you
RAPPORT
I am willing to know you
INTENTION

Chapter 4

Listening

Listening is a rare happening among human beings.
You cannot listen to the word another is speaking
if you are preoccupied with your appearance, or with impressing
the other, or are trying to decide what you are going to say
when the other stops talking, or are debating about whether
what is being said is true or relevant or agreeable.
Such matters have their place, but only after listening to
the word as the word is being uttered. Listening is a
primitive act of love in which a person gives himself to
another's word, making himself accessible and
vulnerable to that word.

— William Stringfellow[39] —

The Power of Reflective Listening

An important indicator of your openness is how you are listening.

Thus, we travel to the next level of the Pyramid, building on Intention, Rapport, and Openness.

In order to ask powerful questions, you need to listen, confirm you are listening correctly, and then show that you understand to the best of your ability. You can ask a question that sounds powerful, but if your intention is not aligned, you have not built rapport, or if you are listening only to be right, the question will lose its power. In order for a question to be truly powerful, it requires you to listen deeply and completely. Only then can you ask a question that offers the power to create something new.

Did you know?

Humans can listen faster than we can speak. The average person talks at a rate of 125–175 words per minute. Even a livestock auctioneer only speaks at around 250–350 words per minute. However, we can listen at a rate of up to 400 words per minute.[40] No wonder it is so easy for our minds to wander!

When we aren't fully present and intentional with our listening, our relationships may merely survive, but this book is about much more than that. As we'll unpack in this chapter, the power of reflective listening is a key ingredient for our relationships, teams, and organizations to thrive.

How do we teach listening? How do we really learn to listen? There is no way to close your ears like you can your mouth—and yet they seem to have an on/off switch. Baltasar Gracián said, "We have eyelids but not earlids, for the ears are the portals of learning, and Nature wanted to keep them wide open."[41] Because we cannot close our ears, we tend to think that we can listen passively (and maybe some of us can).

But I believe in order to ask truly powerful questions, you need to take action. Listening is a verb, after all. To be able to *truly understand* what someone is saying, we are each required to engage the part of our mind that wants to connect to others. Sure, sound waves are bouncing around us all the time and they will hit our eardrums, but it is our duty to march to that drumbeat in a way that engages our whole being. Each of our senses gets engaged in the process.

> *I thought I knew something about the power of listening but a recent failure taught me that I still have a lot to learn. While this book was undergoing the editing process, my company, We and Me Inc.™, had an inbound request for some consulting work. A woman left a voicemail saying she was calling from the "IACP" (no further explanation of the acronym) and was looking for an interactive keynote speaker for a Sunday event in October in Philly. Before returning her call, I went to the IACP website and discovered that the event expected to draw 100,000 attendees and that the International Association for Chiefs of Police (IACP) has a LONG history of conferences going back to the 1800s, not to mention*

700 vendors offering everything from guns to massage therapists. It sounded like it might be useful for them to have a connection-based keynote. I quickly returned the call. After three rings, a woman answered and said, "Oh, thanks for calling. I have a loose end I need to wrap up. Can I call you back in a few minutes?"

"Sure!" I say, and then immediately get sucked into my next project without giving the IACP much further thought.

The next thing I know, the phone is ringing and even though I am not quite prepared to offer my full attention to the woman on the other end, I answer and dive in with run-of-the-mill niceties: "So you must be busy getting ready for this. This is a BIG deal. I know because I once was the Director of Development for the largest sustainable conference on the east coast. I bet you are really busy."

"Yeah, really busy getting everything organized and it's lots of fun," she says.

"So tell me what we can do to help you," I reply while reaching for my pen to take notes.

"Okay," she says. "One of our board members suggested you might be able to help us with our IACP conference in Philly in October with about 500 attendees. We would like to do an interactive keynote to help teams to associate with each other on Sunday morning. We are a membership-based organization with lawyers . . ."

After that, I couldn't hear or understand anything else she was saying. It was like my brain had shut off. I was completely focused on five hundred attendees not equalling the 100,000 I'd read about on their website and lawyers not being police chiefs. The cover of this book pops into my head. Somehow, I focused in and told myself to just listen. "Whatever she is saying is way more important than what you think she should be saying," I reminded myself in my head.

". . . and financial people," she said as I tuned back in, my pen once again moving across paper. "We are focused on collaborative divorce cases. Our goal is to keep the process family focused and settle cases out of court whenever possible. Our team members come from all across the world. They love community and connecting to each other. They are rule-breakers who love to challenge the status quo to make the world a better place."

Fortunately, at that point, she paused, giving me a chance to take a deep breath. I was very confused. I double-checked the incoming message and my notes. Something was not adding up.

"So . . . umm . . . do you have more you want to say, or . . . umm . . . is this a good time for me to ask questions?" I said, the words stumbling from my mouth as I attempted to gather my thoughts.

"I'm good," she said. "Your turn."

"Okay, who was the board member who recommended us?" I said.

She told me, and we talked about how full of life and supportive this mutual acquaintance was. So far, that information matched with the data I had in my mind for IACP. Then I told her I'd missed something somewhere *after lawyers but before financial folks.*

"Oh, that was mental health professionals and child therapists," she said. My pen barely moved because there was still no mention of police chiefs.

At this point I was really puzzled and wondering how police chiefs fit in with lawyers and divorce cases.

"Um . . . I thought this is IACP?" I said.

"Oh, it is," she said.

"But where are the police chiefs?" I said. "Sounds like you are the rule-breakers."

"Oh, do you mean the other IACP?" I could hear the smile in her voice as she said this. "Yes, the police chiefs are having a conference the same weekend in the same building. We are also IACP—The International Association for Collaborative Practice."

"Hold on," I said, looking at my inbound emails. "We and Me Inc.™ has two different inbound requests: One for your IACP and one for the other. The subject line of this email says 'Chiefs of Police.' Same letters, same time, same location and both asking for help."

"Were we first?" she says. "Can we be first, please?"

Then we both break into laughter. What are the chances?

And it was then that I realized where I'd fallen down on the job of exercising my listening skills. I had such strong "listening for" data in my head based on my research for IACP that I couldn't hear any of the words she said once they didn't match up with what I expected to hear.

When you are listening, do you search for the next thing someone will say based on what you are expecting them to say? Most of us are not even aware that we're doing this when it's happening. The eight-pound microprocessors resting between our ears do the searching so rapidly that it's effortless. I wasn't even aware that my listening process wasn't allowing any more data to come through. It was as if my brain wasn't even allowing for the possibility that the IACP that she was referring to existed, simply because I hadn't yet read about it. I could have lost an important client.

Do you sometimes listen in hopes that the person you're chatting with will agree with you? Are you hoping they will say something to compliment you? Do you listen for them to say something that is true, wrong, worthy, etc.? In all of these cases, you're listening for what you expect to hear rather than what is actually being said.

The largest hindrance to our open listening is that we often listen for what we want to hear. Have you ever noticed that the people around you tend to experience the same problems over and over, or that every time a loved one shares something with you, you hear a similar story?

> I have a friend who only comes around when she is having problems with her latest boyfriend. It has gotten so bad that when she shows up at my door, I don't even say, "Hi." I just skip to something like, "What is his name and what did he do this time?"

Do you have anybody in your life with whom you have a similar relationship? A similar way of listening is this:

> *I often listen for how people are wrong and how I would fix them. I know, it is such a limited view, and I'm not proud of it. Yet, I'm learning that if I'm listening for how I am right, then I'm only getting part of the story. A very small part. I am missing a huge part of what is being shared with me. My friend can never show up at my door with a story about how things are going well with her latest boyfriend, for I won't even hear it. I will keep listening and digging around for what is wrong. I must choose to open my listening and understand fully all that is being presented to me. It is a choice that offers a more complete understanding of what is happening around me. As I'm writing this, I'm realizing she has not stopped by in six months. My first thought is, "Must be going okay with her current boyfriend." However, what is more realistic is, who would want to stop by if all they get is, "What's wrong with you?"*

What is something that you listen for? When someone talks to you, how do you give him or her your attention?

It is useful to generate a list of what you are listening for. Just ask yourself, "What do I listen for?" and see what shows up. Write as fast as you can, unfiltered. When you are done, think about what your loved ones listen for, and see which of theirs could be on your list, too. You might be surprised. If you sit with this question for a while, other answers will come to you while in the shower, eating your next meal, and during your next conversation.

I love fixing problems and might even be addicted to it, for the payoff is usually gratifying. I'm not the only one who listens for problems they can fix. Have you noticed how leaders within organizations love fixing problems? They tend to have a knack for coming up with solutions and have been promoted in order to solve bigger and bigger problems. They get an endorphin rush putting out fires. Some even go looking for the next fire they can put out just so they can continually "save the day." They feel needed and useful.

> *This is true for Bob, a CEO whose staff I was coaching and training as he was leading a cultural shift in hopes of reducing fear within the organization. Like many in his position, he focused on fixing the current problems and, as a result, missed the bigger picture. Since being promoted to CEO, Bob had lost the ability to see and listen to what the true problem was. He'd become so far removed from the front line that he no longer had all the information needed to address a problem. In turn, those who were on the front line were becoming increasingly frustrated that they had not been heard and were afraid to pass data up the "authority" chain. As soon as one fire was put out, another ignited, because no one was addressing the core of the problem. Rather than listening for root causes, they were only listening for information about the current fire.*

Part of our brain, the reticular activating system (RAS), learns to focus on small bits of data that we deem important. Have you ever noticed upon buying a new car that suddenly there are many more of that make and model on the road than you ever saw before? It is not as if your local dealer sold one hundred more cars overnight. You did not need that data before, so it went unnoticed. Your choice activated something in your RAS that now makes this bit of data important.

There is an important piece of data my wife can see that I'm blind to, even after she points it out. When we go to the beach, she can find half a dozen shark teeth within minutes. I think it is the coolest thing. I want to find them too. I can walk the same beach right next to her and not find a single one—even when my wife makes a one-foot circle in the sand and tells me there is a shark tooth in the circle. I can sit and stare within the circle for twenty minutes and not find it. My wife grew up with boys, and I'd bet her ability to see shark teeth had lots of value in the currency of play.

Henry David Thoreau was once asked how it was that he was able to find so many arrowheads. Just then, he stooped and picked up an arrowhead from between his feet. He said, "We cannot see anything until we are possessed with the idea of it, take it into our heads—and then we can hardly see anything else."[44]

We can train ourselves to notice certain things around us. When we listen, RAS is focused on finding examples in our world to prove we're right and therefore the other person is wrong. Do you think that this makes us good listeners?

How many of the following are true for you? I listen for . . .

▸ What I know (so what I know is confirmed), and I say, "I know that already!"
▸ Approval (so I know that I am liked), and it answers, "Do I fit in here?" or "Am I valued?"
▸ Next action (so I can know where to go next), and I say, "I can do that!"
▸ What is wrong (so I can fix it), and say, "You know, what you need to do is . . ."

Once when I asked a CEO to be aware of the things he's listening for, he listed things like fairness, accusation, dishonesty, hidden messages, manipulation, winning, being right, and blame. He thought these were the "correct" things to listen for. After exploring deeply what might be going on for him when he listens, he added, "I listen for how people defer to me, how they see me as something successful, and whether or not they got excited when I was speaking. I am listening for fans." He said he wanted to create a team of strong leaders to take his business to the next level. This exercise helped him understand why the leaders he trained always left when they were ready to take the reins themselves. He realized he never created an environment for them to thrive; he had created an environment for them to be his greatest fans. When he left them alone to lead, they left. Now he was in a place where he could name what he was listening for and create an opportunity to listen for more. He was able to listen bigger and deeper and hear more of what his employees needed in order to be great leaders, whether or not he was present.

When you practice deep listening, your mind shifts to the needs of those around you. Your focus is on the person sharing instead of your need to be right. When you're in this space, you hear what's really important. No longer is there a need to prove anything. The need is for them to fully express themselves and for you to receive that.

When this type of listening occurs, there is also a shift in the world of the speaker. When we listen as if someone's life depends on it, something radical can happen. We can listen them *into being*. We listen them into a new space—a space where they can recreate themselves in the current moment. Like a kid with Lego blocks, they can make choices about what they want to build because they are being listened to.

So, listen as if lives depend on it. In a real sense, they do, in much the same way my life was altered by my encounter with the Amish man on the bus that fateful day. His listening and his ability to connect created an opportunity for me to choose a whole new life, one in which my focus was no longer on me and my victimhood. ("Poor me . . . I did not know my parents . . . I was left . . . abandoned.") I could now shift my story and shift my past. I had a new self-understanding that was immediately affirmed, that encouraged me to dedicate myself to serving others. He listened to me without any expectations and was not listening for anything in particular. What would shift in your life, if you were able to listen without listening for anything specific?

Deep listening also contributes to building trust and respect. People want to be heard and understood. It may be the highest calling of our humanity. When we are deeply listened to, we become the most alive. Your compassionate listening is a deep service to those around you, and it may be the greatest gift you can give. If you want to build trust with those around you and within your organization, then learn to practice listening deeply. Let go of the judgment and serve the needs of others by showing up and listening.

Reflective listening is a skill that will allow you to open the door to this deep kind of listening in your life and give you the ability to ask powerful questions. In its truest sense, it is a skill of being able to hold a "mirror" for the other person in such a way that they can listen to and evaluate what they are saying, in much the same way that a physical mirror reflects what is visual. When done right, it allows all of your stories to get out of the way and allows you to get closer to the person who is sharing *their* story.

You can do that by "mirroring" what the other person says is true for them. They see the world with a particular view, and if you can show that view back to them, both of you might have a greater understanding of who each of you are. With this greater understanding, the other person can now make choices that they did not have access to a moment ago. You can access this space through reflective listening. This chapter provides strategies for using the subtleties of this skill in powerful ways.

The basic approach here is to use Reflective Listening Statements, also sometimes called mirror statements. The listener can choose to reflect the other person's words cleanly or in other styles that allow for different nuances.

Elements of Reflective Listening Statements

Reflective Listening Statements have two major parts: what they begin with and what they end with. They usually need some kind of transition between the other person saying their words and you reflecting what they are saying.

Reflective Listening Statements begin with words like:

So . . .
So, you are saying . . .
I'm hearing . . .

You then get to make some choices about how the statement ends, based on which form of Reflective Listening Statement you choose to use. There are four forms of Reflective Listening Statements:

- *Verbatim:* This is the simplest form. You can reflect exactly what the other person is saying, using many of the same words as they did. This is especially useful for clarification, if a particular word surprised you, or if there is a lot of emotion in what they are saying.

- *Translation:* You can reflect what you are hearing the other person say using your own words. Simple Translation uses synonyms for their words. Far Out Translation uses words with different meanings.

- *Unstated Feelings:* You can reflect your sense of the other person's feelings, even if they are not being said directly.

- *Connecting the Dots:* You can connect the different ideas that the other person is sharing.

The following tables may help you identify and create each of the reflective listening styles. Then, let's explore each of these types of Reflective Listening Statements in detail.

Reflective Listening Statements begin with:		And end with:
A Transition Phrase Like		**Verbatim**
So, you are wondering . . .	You are feeling . . .	Using many of their words
You believe . . .	It sounds like you really value . . .	**Translation**
So, you are thinking about . . .	It's interesting that . . .	*Simple*—in your own words using synonyms of their words
I hear you saying . . .	So, what I'm hearing . . .	*Far Out*—using your own words with expanded meanings
So, what you are saying is . . .	I believe what you're saying is that . . .	
So . . .	I'm noticing . . .	**Unstated Feelings**
You seem . . .	It's almost like you said . . .	Giving their feelings back to them even if they did not say them, by paying attention to body language and tone
I'm getting . . .	I'm observing . . .	
You think . . .	I sense . . .	
It is important to you . . .	Are you saying . . .	
It feels like you are . . .	So, your opinion is . . .	
What I'm understanding is . . .	Your experience has been . . .	
It sounds to me like . . .	I'm getting the impression . . .	**Connecting the Dots**
You sound as if you are . . .	I'm getting the sense that . . .	Tying together ideas and thoughts they have shared over time into one reflection
Sounds like . . .	When you say this . . . I'm hearing that . . .	
From your perspective . . .	This is what I'm hearing you say . . .	
I'm picking up . . .		
It seems as though . . .		

Verbatim Reflective Listening Statements

Your goal is simply to give the speaker back what they are putting out into the world. As the mirror is for the visual world, you become the reflector of their words. Use this when:

- you don't understand what they are trying to get across
- you are surprised by the words they are using
- you're not sure of the actual words they are using (due to accent)
- repeating the words would be useful for others in the room
- you're unsure why they are sharing this bit of information
- you want them to know that you heard them (but maybe did not understand them)
- it would be useful for them to clarify

For example:

> Jose is saying, "I don't understand why people are so inconsiderate. They are supposed to be professionals and yet they don't care what I say."

First, you need a starting transition phrase. Let's use "I hear you saying . . ."

Now you add what you heard Jose say, using his words.

> "So, Jose, I hear you saying these professionals are inconsiderate and they don't care."

Or "You're saying that professionals don't care what you say."

Or "You're wondering why professionals can be inconsiderate and don't care what you say."

Translation Reflective Listening Statements

Translation is basically asking, "I am understanding XYZ, do I have that right?" by taking the other person's words, digesting them as your own, and giving them back to the other person.

A *Simple Translation* is giving the other person's words back to them after you have digested them and understood them. In Simple Translation, you may use synonyms. For example:

Jose says, "I don't understand why people are so inconsiderate. They are supposed to be professionals and yet they don't care what I say."

The word "inconsiderate" jumps out for you. Some other words that have similar meaning are unsympathetic, rude, disrespectful, and thoughtless. Therefore, you pick one that seems to be close to what he is saying and give it back to him.

"So, Jose, you feel like you get an unsympathetic ear?"

Or "It sounds like the professionals were rude to you."

Or, it might be a little bit more of a stretch, but you could say "So Jose, I'm hearing that you have been mistreated."

If the words "don't care" struck you, you then might proceed with:

> "You're saying that people who get paid to do a job should also be able to listen to your concerns."

> *Or* "You wish these folks would be a little more attentive to your needs."

With a *Far Out Translation*, you're stepping out on a limb to see how far their world extends with the words they are saying and how BIG the truth is of their statement. How far out does their statement extend to other parts of their world? For example:

> "I'm getting the impression that the company has some bad hiring practices."

> *Or* "I'm hearing you say that they should fire all the customer service reps."

Another way to think about Far Out Translation is to take an arrow (their translated words) and try to hit the target (the core or heart of their message). Often, we try to hit the bull's eye of the target dead center (with Verbatim or Simple Translation reflections), but with Far Out Translation, we deliberately try to hit somewhere outside of the center of the target—maybe closer to the edge, maybe just a ring or two out from the center of the bull's eye, or maybe off the edge of the target completely. You become an explorer trying to find the edge of their message, exploring what is true and not true for them with as little judgment as possible. You're just exploring and seeing how the world occurs for them. What is a story they are telling themselves that they believe to be true?

Using a Far Out Translation might venture into territory that is not true for them. That is okay, and they will help you clear it up. In the example, you might think that Jose values politeness.

A Far Out Translation might be:

> "It sounds like you really value politeness and that no one who gets paid for what they are doing should be so rude."

> Jose might respond: "It's not politeness that I'm concerned about. I want directness! When they say they can fix it, and yet send me on a run-around that only makes it worse, it drives me crazy. Why can't they just be honest and say they cannot fix it or have never dealt with this problem before?"

I often use this type of reflective listening when I'm trying to see how the speaker's words fit into their whole worldview. I might know (or think I know) something about their worldview and I'm trying to find out if their words match with that world. Far Out reflective listening is not something that I do often, and a few arrows (reflections) might fall short of the target or even miss completely. However, I include this type of reflective listening here because when I do use it, it seems like the most perfect tool for the moment. When it works, it can help the conversation move to a deeper and more meaningful place quickly, and bring a crisp clarity to what we are talking about, especially if I have established good rapport.

Unstated Feelings: Reflective Listening Statements

Reflecting Unstated Feelings allows the other person to know they have been heard on a deeper level. Reflective listening at this level unveils unsaid emotions in the speaker that may even be unknown to them. In order to reflect Unstated Feelings, you must be listening with your whole being.

You are listening with your ears for change in tone of voice, as well as a change in tempo or speed. A higher tone with a quick tempo might suggest excitement. A lower tone with slower tempo might suggest confusion or uncertainty about what they are sharing.

You are listening with your eyes. What is the person doing with their body that might be an indication of some underlying feeling that has not been stated yet? The message expressed with their body language can tell you more than their words can.

Your other senses might be useful, too, for listening at this level. We will cover this in more detail in the section on empathy.

For example:

What do you notice while Jose is speaking? "I don't understand why people are so inconsiderate. They are supposed to be professionals and yet they don't care what I say."

Let's say you notice that he has clenched his fist and his jaw muscles have tightened. You know from your own experience that when you do these things you are feeling frustrated or maybe disrespected, so you assume that he's feeling that way as well. You check that assumption by saying,

> "So you are feeling really frustrated in the way you were treated."

Or "You feel that people should be treated with dignity and heard. And you were not."

Notice that Jose did not say "frustrated" or "dignity." You are taking a risk by adding your deeper understanding of what is not being expressed in words. If you have done a good job with establishing rapport, he can accept or deny what you are saying. Most likely, he will appreciate that you are listening to all of him.

Connecting the Dots

Connecting the Dots could also be called Connecting the Ideas, although Connecting the Dots is more accurate because you might be connecting more than just ideas. Connecting the Dots requires you to listen to all of the data that you are receiving and share any connections that you are making. You are listening for more than just the other person's words. You are listening for how their ideas, concepts, and body language are congruent or incongruent with what is being said. What connections are you making based on what they are saying? With Connecting the Dots, you will share those connections as you see them.

For example, you might say the following to Jose:

> "Earlier you said that these folks were 'cheap' and now you're saying they are 'inconsiderate.' You want to make sure you don't work with them again."

Or "Based on all that you have said, you are 'done' with them. And you want to make sure this does not happen to you again."

Or, in an incongruent way: "Earlier you were talking about how much you love these people and now you are saying that they are so 'inconsiderate.'" (You could follow this reflecting with "What happened?" Just pointing out the two different dots might be enough for them to reflect.)

Listening in this way can be so profound for the other person that sometimes you need to ask for permission before sharing. You might say, "I am making some connections with what you are saying. Would you mind if I share?" If they say, "Okay," then go ahead and share. If they indicate they would prefer you not share, then move on.

When you are Connecting the Dots, you can provide a great service for someone. You have offered another brain to examine their perspective in a way that they aren't able to. By sharing your perspective, you give them a new vantage point from which to see their lives.

So, what is the advantage of reflective listening? The largest advantage of reflective listening is that it helps the other person engage with you in a way that advances the conversation in much the same way a gear connects with another gear to propel a machine forward.

When two or more people come together, one person can begin to spin gears without engaging with anyone else. Sure, they might be talking, but nothing is being shared because they have not engaged with anyone. They have not connected. When a listener uses reflective listening, they engage themselves so that deeper and more complete understanding can happen for all parties. This is done by giving the speaker their own words or ideas back to them to ask subconsciously, "Is this what we are talking about? Did I get it right?" If the response is "yes," then more information can be added to the conversation. If the answer is "no," then WONDERFUL! The speaker can clarify immediately, and the conversation can move from a place of disconnection to a place of connection, from a place of confusion to a place of clarity, from a place of ignorance to a place of understanding. Therefore, as a result of using reflective listening, you have made a movement toward understanding, which creates room for empathy (we'll get to that more in the next chapter). Due to reflective listening, one person can see how the other sees the world in that moment. Remember, in true reflective listening, your goal is not to seek understanding to get your point across. It is the antithesis of that. Using reflective listening allows the listener to see the world as the speaker sees the world, with the added benefit of gaining insight into themselves as well.

Another way to think about this is to see a map of a city. You likely want to know where you are on the map. If there is not a

"You are here" dot, then you need to do some work. First, you need to find landmarks around you in the real world and see if they exist on the map. In the same way, reflective listening can allow others to know, "Ah, that road is over there, and that park is here, so we must be here!" or "She thinks race is the primary factor we all use to judge people's ability, and he believes race is irrelevant." The conversation to have is the one where those two ideas intersect.

▶ Trap: Repeating the reflection style

When people pick up reflective listening as a tool to ask better questions, I commonly see this Trap. Either they use the same transition phrase again and again, or they use the same form of reflective statements, when something else would better suit the speaker. The two most common forms people use when learning are Verbatim and Simple Translation. This is a result of doing what is comfortable and easy or a fear of reflecting the wrong thing.

▶ Tool: Change it up and take a risk

The simple Tool for this Trap is to continue to change up your reflective listening style. Focus on listening and really absorbing what is being said. When it's your turn to reflect, take the time to breathe and give back exactly what you heard. Take a chance to explore the unknown territory and do a Far Out Translation, Unstated Feelings, or Connecting the Dots style of reflection. For some, it feels very risky. Students who are slow to use reflective listening often say things like, "I don't want to put words in their mouth" or "If I reflect wrong they will think I'm not a good listener." Fear is holding them back from connecting and fully understanding what the speaker is expressing.

If you keep using the same transition phrase—"I am hearing you say . . ." for example—you will sound like a robot. People will notice and be less receptive to your words. Although only a few are listed above, there are hundreds of ways to start a reflective statement. Sure, you might have some phrases that you lean on and use more often. That is okay, but it is important to be well-versed in other starting phrases so that you can be fluid in your transition. Try using new ones even if you are unsure how they will work. Take a risk. What will it sound like if you say, "So you're wondering if . . ."

Also, take a risk in moving between all the different forms of reflective statements. If you only use Verbatim and Simple Translation, then people will feel like they are talking to a parrot. The reason I have taken the time to break down these different forms of reflective statements is to give my students the ability to move between the different forms with ease. Using Verbatim may be perfect in a particular moment, and at other times, it might be more useful to Connect the Dots or share what Unstated Feelings you are picking up on. None of these forms are better than the other. There are times when one form will be the most appropriate choice for that particular moment. You won't know when that moment is unless you practice moving between all the different forms.

Each of the reflective listening styles allows you to access the speaker's truth from different directions. For example, I have found that when emotions are really high, it is best to give the person exactly what they have said back to them (Verbatim).

However, when they are in a place of self-reflection and are ready to explore some yet unknown truth about themselves, Connecting the Dots can be a tool that opens up a whole new room inside of them.

Did you know?

Physicians, on average, interrupt 70 percent of patient interviews within eleven seconds of the patient beginning to speak.[45] As a result, only 36 percent of patients feel they were able to fully put their concerns on the table. In doing research for the book, we spoke with one emergency room physician, Dr. John, who had attended a training on increasing patient satisfaction scores. The trainer had suggested an interesting tip to increase patient satisfaction: don't saying anything for the first sixty seconds of the conversation. He shared with us that this simple shift helped to increase his patient satisfaction scores. But he also said, "It is amazing to me how much more focused and interested in my questions or insights my patients are after even one minute of me listening to them." Better scores *and* better outcomes all from only forty-nine extra seconds of intentional listening.

When you add in the *reflective* listening piece to all that we've been discussing, you have a recipe for your patients, students, coworkers, customers, spouses, and kids to really feel seen, heard, and understood. Like you "get them."

Self-work question: What do you think your "second count" would be at work—more or less than eleven seconds? How about at home? If you doubled the time that you listened before interjecting, how might your "relationship satisfaction" scores go up?

▶ Tool: Ask permission

For some, the following three forms of reflective statements can feel risky: Far Out Translation, Unstated Feelings, and Connecting the Dots. These three forms tend to move the conversation to a new place. (In contrast, Verbatim and Simple Translation tend to keep the conversation where it is.) This is true if the conversation is one-on-one or in a group. For the person getting ready to reflect, it can feel risky and scary to move to this new place. One thing you can do to "check in" with yourself is to ask, "Is this risk in alignment with the group's intentions?" If yes, you can then ask for permission. Permission might sound like, "I would like to reflect back something that I'm hearing, but it feels a bit risky; would it be okay with you if I reflect back what I'm hearing from you?" You need to be okay with them saying no, and if they say yes, then give them what you been hearing: "Okay, so what I'm understanding is . . ."

▶ Trap: Failure to confirm when you know it will be useful

Reflective listening can be powerful when done well but can be limiting when poorly executed or when you miss the mark by not getting the whole story. When using Reflective Listening Statements, it's important to pay attention to the feedback the speaker is giving you about your statement. You used reflective listening to offer what you think you heard, and sometimes your reflection doesn't match what the person meant to say. Let me share an experience where I failed to confirm that I got the reflection right.

During a three-day intensive course, a student became the teacher. In a dialogue about being impeccable with your words and the power of words, a young man, Bryan, was sharing a story about being abused as a child and told he was worthless. It became obvious to the group that he had a dysfunctional and violent family life. Later in the dialogue, he shared that when he grew older, people told him that his thoughts or ideas did not matter. I got a clear picture of what his life must have been like in these stories and was impressed by how he was able to be so vulnerable (something new for him) in this new group of people. Although the conversation was flowing, I felt a strong need to tell him that I understood and to affirm his ability to share. I paused the group for a moment, told the person who was then speaking that she would be able to continue in just a moment, and looked deeply in Bryan's eyes. I could feel his pain and felt tears forming on the bottom of my eyes. I wanted to reflect back what he was placing in the dialogue so he would know that someone understood. "Bryan, I get it. You have been told your whole life that you are wrong, that you do not matter, and that your thoughts are not worth sharing. I got it." I sent it with all the love I could muster in the moment and asked the last speaker to continue. As I sat back to listen to the next speaker, I felt a small tightness in my chest and wondered, "Did he get that I got it?" but pushed the thought away and focused on facilitating the group. I was more concerned about moving the conversation along than confirming if my reflection landed where I intended it to land. I failed to confirm if my reflection was accurate even though my chest tightened and I felt uneasy about how I had reflected Bryan's words. I pushed those feelings aside for the sake of the flow of the conversation and invited the conversation to move forward. I now wonder how things might have been different if I had opted to confirm with Bryan what I had heard by saying something along the lines of, "Am I understanding you correctly?"

The next day, after the class had covered reflective listening in detail, Bryan came to me with a question. I answered it, and before he turned to leave I said, "It's my turn, I have a question." I started to say what I was trying to send him in that moment the day prior, but could not, as my words got all tangled up. Then I asked, "Remember that moment yesterday when I was reflecting about your life? What was I trying to say to you?" He said flippantly, "Oh, you were telling me that I was being too vulnerable and sharing too much. That is why I did not share for the rest of the dialogue."

My chin dropped to the floor. "I knew something in that moment was not right. That is why you did not share anymore?"

"Yep!"

"Do you know what was going on for me? Did you see my face? Did you see the tears in my eyes?"

"Nope."

"I am glad we are talking about this. In that moment, I was sending you all the love I could muster, for you have been told your whole life that you are wrong. I was trying to say I got that. That it must be hard living a life in which all that you encounter tells you that you are wrong."

He smiled as learning settled in. I continued: "However, do you see that you are so attuned to listen for 'I am wrong,' that when the total opposite is stated, still all you can hear is, 'I am wrong?'"

His face lit up. He understood that his whole past came into the present in such a way that he had made the present look just like the past. When love came to him in the present he translated it as "I'm wrong," in the same way he'd grown accustomed to doing his entire life. When I referred back to the moment the previous day, he responded by being flippant as if he was saying, "Ya I know . . . I was wrong . . . but you see . . . I fixed it by not sharing for the rest of the dialogue."

What is most sad to me about this story is that he lost a day in the retreat to be truly himself based on my inaction. My reflection was interpreted as discipline and he clammed right up. He could have had more useful time in the workshop if I had slowed down just a bit more and listened more deeply to the tightening of my chest.

The next day during a group dialogue, Bryan was able to open up again. He shared what it was like for people to call him horrible names related to his sexual orientation. "I hate it when people call me a ----." He was able to be vulnerable because he knew that I was on his team, which in turn allowed the entire group to do meaningful work and contribute to making a difference.

▸ Antidote: Confirm when you're thinking "I know"

If you sense your reflection did not land correctly, it can be useful to confirm that you have, indeed, hit the mark. There are lots of ways to confirm but the most direct is the following tool.

▸ Tool: Ask, "Did I get it right?"

After delivering your Reflective Listening Statement, pause for a moment and ask if your reflection is accurate. There are many ways you can do this, such as "Did I get it right?" or "I'm not sure I completely got what you are saying. Would you tell me more so I can make sure I'm clear on what you're saying?"

▸ Trap: "I have to get it right"

When people start using reflective listening, they sometimes get so caught up in getting the reflection "right" that they don't do it at all or they stick to what is safe. In this case, "right" might mean feeling like you need to hit the target squarely in the center. You don't have to get it "right." You just need to be heading in that direction.

▸ Tool: Trust your rapport

If your intention is clear and you have established rapport, most of the time people will correct you if you don't have the reflection right. Alternatively, they will add more to their story because you did get it right and they feel like they were heard. Either way contributes to greater understanding. So trust your rapport and reflect back what you heard, even if you are not sure you got it right. The conversation will be better because you did.

How Listening Can Be Applied in Groups

Another advantage of reflective listening in group dialogue is that it gives the facilitator a tool for pushing the conversation forward or keeping the conversation in the same place for a while, if need be. Often, we think a facilitator's job is to get the conversation to a deep and meaningful place. Though that might be true, it is also a facilitator's job to stall the conversation to prevent it from going astray or moving too quickly, if that is what is most useful for the group. This might be necessary if emotions are running high, if people are skirting around an issue that needs to be addressed, or if it is obvious that not everyone in the room is understanding what is being said. Reflective listening early on can help determine that everyone is starting in the same place.

If it is early in a dialogue and the facilitator has a meaningful question, it is beneficial for the group to hear as many individual answers as possible before delving into any one response. You want to make sure everyone is on the train before leaving the station. If you ask a question and one or two people answer and you immediately move the conversation to a deeper place (maybe by asking those people deeper open-ended questions), then the train might leave without everyone on board. However, if you use reflective statements (especially Verbatim or Simple Translation), and then ask for others to answer the question as well, everyone gets to see (or contribute) before the train takes off.

It is also useful if the facilitator can reflect to the group as a whole, using reflective statements such as Simple Translation or Connecting the Dots. Then the group can collectively see and understand the world which they are about to traverse.

What is an issue that you think not enough people are talking about?

What is one thing life is teaching you right now?

Summary of Listening

Reflective listening allows for:

- the listener to engage actively with the speaker
- better understanding between all parties
- building empathy
- clarification of ideas so that all parties have a clearer idea of what is being said

Did you know?

Listening well is quite a challenge for human beings, even though recent research has discovered that we start listening ten weeks before we are even born![46]

Even though we spend a good chunk of our lives listening, deep listening expert Oscar Trimboli suggests only 2 percent of us have been trained in how to listen. As the previous story demonstrates, listening and reflective listening takes a bit of deliberate practice. Our brains are wired to listen with a me-centered focus to defend, fix, win, etc. The self-work section below provides some quick and clever ways to join the 2 percent of trained listeners.

Remember, the way we listen has the power to change what people say. If we don't like what someone is saying or how they are saying it, how might we use the tools in this chapter to listen and reflect to create a conversation that matters?

If you want to dive a bit deeper into this, you can access free tips and a behind-the-scenes video from us on the power of listening at **www.weand.me/listening**.

Self-Work for Listening

Use reflective listening in a relationship in which you feel you know the other person well and think you know how the person sees the world. When I practiced this with my mom, I gained a greater understanding of how she sees the world. This would not have been possible before.

You might enjoy having questions prepared that you can use at a moment's notice, so that you can reflect their answers. You can use the Notice, Wonder, and Inquire model, as shared in a previous chapter on Rapport, to pick something they are wearing, carrying, or sharing, and ask about it. On the other hand, you could just ask a question spontaneously. You are already collecting and creating powerful questions that invite authenticity, vulnerability, and openness. These types of questions often will not have a correct answer—just an answer that will invite more curiosity.

Here are a few of mine. You can borrow one if you like:

- What brings you joy?
- What is this moment (or life) teaching you, right now?
- What are you curious about?
- What is your biggest challenge?

Using reflective statements with the strangers who show up in your life can be fun too. You will quickly gain a deeper understanding of who they are. Go see for yourself.

Create your own list of things that you listen for. Keep a little journal or make a note in your phone. When you hear or see something that you can identify as a "listening for," make a note of it. Watch your list grow.

The power comes later when you're in a conversation. You can simply ask, "What am I listening for?" and you will have access to listening to more of what is being shared and not be trapped by the veil of only what you are listening for.

It is important to note that it will not serve you to judge what you are listening for as either good or bad. They just *are*—let them be. They have served you up to this point in your life. The value of paying attention to what you are listening for is to expand what you are able to listen to so you can listen more fully.

With you!
EMPATHY
I get you
LISTENING
I hear you
OPENNESS
I see you
RAPPORT
I am willing to know you
INTENTION

Chapter 5

Empathy

Self-absorption in all its forms kills empathy, let alone compassion. When we focus on ourselves, our world contracts as our problems and preoccupations loom large. But when we focus on others, our world expands. Our own problems drift to the periphery of the mind and so seem smaller, and we increase our capacity for connection—or compassionate action.

— Daniel Goleman, *Social Intelligence: The New Science of Human Relationships*[47] —

The Power of Connection

Empathy is a powerful place from which to ask questions. Let's travel up to the final layer of the Pyramid and explore what it might look like to ask a question from a place of Empathy. How we look at empathy might surprise you, for it might not be what you expect. In order to understand how powerful empathy can be, we need to understand what happens when we ask questions from two other common places: Apathy and Sympathy. First, here is a story that will illustrate the difference between apathy, sympathy, and empathy (adapted from Mike Bagshaw[48]).

Imagine that you and a friend have been given a two-night stay at a remote cabin in upstate New York in December. You are excited to explore the Finger Lakes region and as you arrive at the cabin, you want to have a cup of tea before exploring. Your friend, however, is ready to explore now and heads outside to put on his snowshoes. You sit down at the huge picture window to enjoy the view of the fields, lake, and forest.

As you're looking out the window, you notice your friend snowshoeing across the field and playing in the snow. He walks across the frozen lake and suddenly disappears. He has fallen through the ice.

What do you do? Do you go to his aid, do you run, do you grab something, do you call for help? What is it that you would do? Think about it for a moment before you read on—the answer might surprise you.

For the sake of this story, let's say there are three alternatives.

The first option is to continue to sit and enjoy your tea. This seems like an unfeeling choice if he is your friend—but can you agree that it is a possibility? Maybe this is not a choice you would make, but it's an option nonetheless. You would stay right where you are, enjoy your tea, and observe what is happening. "What is happening now? I see some water splashing . . . ah, it looks like his head's going underwater . . . it appears as if he is trying to take his snowshoes off . . ." The whole time, you are only observing what is happening from the comfort of your chair.

The second option is to jump out of the chair, maybe drop your tea in the process, and bolt out the door. This sounds like a good idea, right? Let's see how it plays out. You run across the field, onto the ice, and as you get close enough to help him, you, too, fall in. You are now in the ice-cold water and you begin to feel the cold chill your bones. You are now feeling the same as your friend; although he has felt it for some minutes longer, you are quickly catching up. The chill factor is increasing quickly. You and your friend are feeling the same thing.

The third option is to jump out of your seat, call for help if possible, grab something that you could use to rescue him with (rope, perhaps) and a blanket, and then head out the door. When you get to the lake, you stop where the ice is still solid or maybe even stay on the bank. Then you stretch out and offer what you brought to rescue your friend. You encourage him to pull himself out of the water while you continue to stand on solid ground. When your friend gets out of the water, you offer him the warmth of the blanket and celebrate the presence of terra firma.

Each of these options is a real possibility. A few things might be different in real life, but let's allow the story to teach us how we might ask questions. Each scenario represents either Apathy, Sympathy, or Empathy.

Apathy

In the first option, you were noticing just the facts. You witnessed what was happening with no emotion and simply observed, making a mental list of what happened. You were not part of the story but just watching the story as it occurred around you. The picture window in front of you is more like a TV depicting your friend's world. You are watching and you are unengaged.

Apathy-searching questions are commonplace—they are asked with the expectation of garnering factual answers. When we think of people like detectives, journalists, and lawyers, it brings to mind an image of someone who wants "just the facts, ma'am"—no other information or additional interpretation is needed. Asking fact-searching questions is limiting.

Examples of fact-gathering questions are:

▸ Where did this happen?
▸ Who was involved?
▸ How long did it take?

When we ask questions like this, we are asking them from a place of apathy. We are interested in the facts, and little else.

Sometimes we need a few facts to give context to the story the other person is sharing. However, more often than not, asking a powerful question will prompt the person to include the facts that you need to paint a full picture.

It is important to note that asking fact-searching questions can be useful to clear up confusion. For instance, did others in the room exhibit body language or make a statement that suggests they do not understand? If so, you can ask a clear, short, fact-searching question to alleviate misunderstanding. Fact-searching questions can also be useful early in a conversation or connection because they may bring some data into the conversation that allows for deeper understanding (usually with follow-up questions). However, get away from fact-searching questions as quickly as possible. They are tools in your toolbox but should not be used as often as we tend to use them.

Apathetic questions will elicit an expected response. This is especially true when the person who is asking the question is making a judgment or if they are not connected to the issue or person. When we are in a place of judgment, there's a rift between the people involved in the conversation. This chasm will not be closed by asking more fact-searching questions. However, asking empathetic questions (those without judgment) will help you close the divide and understand the whole story.

Sympathy

Let's explore the second option in the story. In this case, in an attempt to be useful, you, too, have fallen through the ice and you feel the cold just as your friend does. We are going to call that sympathy. When sympathy appears in a conversation, you find yourself feeling the same as the person telling you their story, and you may lose your own footing. Perhaps their story sounds so much like yours that you become unaware of what the other person is feeling, and instead you are feeling what the story reminds you of in your own story. You are now in an illusion. You think you are listening to the other person, but really, you are listening to yourself. While they tell their story, you are hearing your own. You have become lost in the story and can often no longer separate your own story from the story of the person you are listening to.

> *For many years, I asked questions from a place of sympathy, and thought that I was doing a service as I listened. I still interact from this place from time to time—it happens. However, I have found that sympathy is frequently a trap. In that sympathetic place, I can never ask truly great questions for anyone else but myself. This is a place where powerful questions are generated for myself but not for the other person.*

With sympathetic questions, you get lost in emotions. Between what you're feeling and what they're feeling, emotions become so entangled that you are no longer able to facilitate any kind of self-realization. In extreme cases, you are crying, and you think you are crying for them, but the tears derive from your own pain. Your questions come from what would be best for you, not what would be best for them.

It feels good to commiserate with someone, to show them that you are capable of the same feelings they are and want to bear their pain. We often fall into this place of sympathy because we believe this is how to be good listeners. Here, we are already in the icy water, shivering with the friend, instead of being in a position to pull them out.

Empathy

If you exercise the third option in the ice story, you know that your friend is cold and struggling, and you know that you are on solid ground. From that solid ground, you can be more helpful than if you also fall into the frigid water. You throw a line (of connection) from that solid ground and help your friend save himself. In asking powerful questions, you are able to hold two places in your mind and heart at once: both the importance of the solid ground (firmly rooted in the truth with the big picture in mind) and the effects of the cold water (the emotional storm that the other is in). You can feel their pain (or joy) without getting lost in it. You are informed by your prior experience of being cold and understand what that feels like, and yet you do not have to physically feel it in order to convey that you comprehend what it means to be cold. Knowledge of the solid ground gives you leverage. From that place, you can have two vantage points: your own and theirs. Often just seeing their perspective is enough for the connection to be real and useful for all involved. There is no need to fix it or make it right. The solid ground offers a place that allows you to ask questions that help shed light on their situation.

Choosing empathy allows the relationship to move toward connection, allowing for compassionate action. Apathy and sympathy can have the opposite effect and actually pull people apart. Apathy moves the relationship to a dry wasteland in which only part of the person is invited to show up. With sympathy, everyone is so awash in their own feelings that they are not able to take on anyone's perspective but their own.

Asking questions from a place of empathy is truly an art. It is difficult to describe in words alone and can only be refined with practice. Below are some hints to make the practice easier.

Colloquially speaking, we speak of empathy as walking in

someone else's shoes. Using the icy pond story, this definition does not quite match.

So, then, what is empathy? In short, it is being grounded in what you know to be true and understanding what is not just true for you, but also true for them. It would be more accurate to say, "I walk in one of your shoes while also walking in one of mine." You have an understanding (or a shared experienced) of their world, while maintaining an understanding of your own.

This is the real, true power of empathy. Instead of sitting across from someone, you sit beside them and look out from the same perspective they do. Sometimes you might do this physically, but you *must* move in this way mentally if you desire to be empathic.

Did you know?

The term "empathy" was first introduced in 1909 by psychologist Edward B. Titchener as a translation of the German term *einfühlung* (meaning "feeling into").

We think the graphic below is a beautiful articulation of the German origin. When we move beyond apathy or sympathy and partially "feel into" another person's world, a separate and disconnected "you" and "me" (or even "you" versus "me") can become "we."

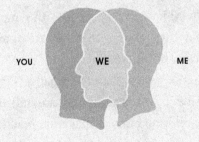

YOU   WE   ME

In relation to reflective listening, if you desire to be empathic, strive to reflect back the world as they see it, with as little judgment as possible. You're a clean mirror, allowing them to see themselves through their own words—regardless of whether you agree with them or not. This is the hard part—mirroring back their image exactly as they express it without polluting that image with any of your ideas.

> Once, I was sharing a story with a woman who was a near stranger about a dynamic that I was having with my mother. I knew I was heard in an empathic way when the woman said to me, "You are wondering if your mom is crazy" (Far Out Translation Reflective Listening Statement). That response was shocking to me. Not because the statement was untrue but because of how very true it was in that moment. There was nothing I had said that would make it easy for her to see that. I did not use the words "crazy" or "wondering." All I had said was, "My mom was cold about going on this trip before she went, and as soon as she left on the trip, she gave me a call and was super excited." How did the woman come up with "So you are wondering if your mom is crazy?" without me saying so? She was able to listen to me in an empathic way. She also reflected to confirm she was understanding my story.

In relation to open-ended questions, you can build on the reflection you've provided and then ask an open question that gives both you and the other person more clarity of their world—again, with as little judgment as possible.

Summary of Apathy, Sympathy, and Empathy:

Apathy	focus on facts
Sympathy	focus on feelings and the "music behind the words"
Empathy	focus on: ▸ the whole story ▸ their personality ▸ how they see the world ▸ their background ▸ what they fear ▸ what they aspire to ▸ what story they are telling themselves about who they are

Did you know?

Human brains are wired for empathy. Nearly everyone has had the experience of flinching when observing another person in pain, such as when someone's hand is slammed in a car door.[49] Neuroscientists attribute this instinctual, empathetic flinch to specific neurons in our brain called "mirror neurons."

More than two decades ago, a team of Italian researchers discovered mirror neurons while observing monkeys' brains. They noticed that certain cells activated both when a monkey performed an action and when that monkey watched another monkey perform the same action.[50]

For the times that empathy doesn't come so naturally, the tool below is invaluable.

▶ Tool: Describe their world

What can you do if you find it difficult to be empathetic? It can be exhausting, and sometimes we convince ourselves that we are unable to stand in the place of empathy in order to make things easier on ourselves. If you feel lost (or you feel that it is difficult to be empathetic) and seemingly cannot find an empathetic place within yourself from which to ask powerful questions, I suggest, *Describe the world as they see it.*

Share with them a description of how they see the world. It is as if you've become the narrator, standing offstage, sharing with them and the audience how their life is occurring to them in this present moment. Your focus is on them. Combined with your desire to ask powerful, affecting questions, this Tool is a doorway to an empathetic world.

Asking yourself these questions might help you streamline your description:

- ▸ How do they see the world?
- ▸ How do they see themselves in that world?
- ▸ How does the world push on them?
- ▸ How do they define themselves in this world?
- ▸ Who are they willing to be and who are they *not* willing to be?

Reflect back their description of their world. If you need an easy way to do it, it might be best to use Verbatim style. If you think you can reflect without judgment, then do a Simple Translation. If you feel confused about what they've said, feel lost about what to say to them, or are having a strong emotional response yourself, this might not be the best time to do the other styles (Far Out Translation, Connecting the Dots, or Unstated Feelings). When you are feeling this way, your own judgments might sneak into your statement and it will be less about them and more about you.

▶ Trap: You find yourself saying, "They are wrong"

You think they are wrong. "I cannot describe the world as they see it if they are wrong!"

If you are thinking the other person is wrong, who are you thinking about? Yourself! Rather than listening openly, you are listening to satisfy your own need to be right. In that moment, you are no longer being empathic. You have found the judgment and you are basking in it. If you find that your inner dialogue or your spoken words are loaded with judgment, or you find that you're telling yourself the speaker is wrong (or that your view is right), then you have fallen into a trap. This might seem like you're offering a Far Out Translation and saying something they did not say just so you can prove a point. For example:

Sam says, "I think we should move all our staff out of the offices, let them work from home, and meet digitally. That way, we won't have to worry about office space."

Lynne thinks to herself that this is a ridiculous idea and asks, "Are you saying that you want to quit?"

Can you hear that Lynne is trying to prove a point or trying to prove that is Sam is wrong? She is not really listening for what is underneath what Sam is saying. She is not reflecting the challenge that Sam is up against. She might even be a bit sarcastic to prove her point.

> *A note about sarcasm:* Sometimes when I feel the other person is wrong, I will begin to use sarcastic comments rather than actually confronting what is really happening. I used to love to use sarcasm, and it was pointed out to me that it is off-putting to people, except those who also love sarcasm. My response was, "Everyone loves sarcasm." That response was a window into how I saw the world, for I grew up with abundant sarcasm. A childhood friend of my brother's has told me that he would come to our house just to watch sarcastic comments zing around the room. It was entertaining to him. The word sarcasm comes from the Greek *sarkazein*, which means to "tear flesh." When you look *sarcasm* up in a thesaurus, you see words like mockery, ridicule, and scorn.

Those words don't sound very welcoming to me. So now, I avoid using sarcasm as a way of connecting with people, or when deep work is needed, unless it is clear that I'm being sarcastic toward an object and not a person. Sometimes I still slip up and when I do, I try to say something to them that acknowledges the pain, even if it was funny. "Oops, that was hurtful. I'm sorry. I'm trying to be less sarcastic and I was taught at a young age to rip others apart. Sorry." I think it is no coincidence that my dyslexic brain always tries to spell sarcasm with a "scar" in it, **scar**asm. I'm learning that my sarcastic comments can leave a scar of some sort, and I'm working on letting that go. The benefits have been worth it.

▶ Antidote: They are the expert of their experience

Let the speaker be the expert. They have knowledge about something you do not—specifically, how they came to understand the world.

Often when you find yourself being judgmental (and not empathic), it is because you "know" or "have it all figured out (and that poor soul has not)." You have learned something and know better than they do. However, there is always one thing they are the expert in that you will never understand unless you open your eyes, ears, and your heart: they are the sage in *their* life! They are the expert and the authority in how they came to be in the world. They show up every day in a way that you do not, and they have the greatest understanding of that. Be humble for a moment and see if you can learn from them. Let them be the teacher and ask questions (or listen reflectively), which will give both of you a better understanding of their world. This is a good time to let your natural, genuine curiosity rule and discover how they see themselves in this great big world. Allow yourself to learn something new.

In summary, the antidote has two parts:

1. Know that they are right (from their own perspective).
2. Find something in what they are sharing that you are curious about and follow it.

Did you know?

Empathy has been shown to increase student test scores.

The Collaborative for Academic, Social, and Emotional Learning (CASEL) reports that students who participated in social and emotional learning (SEL) programs that emphasize and teach empathy showed an average gain on achievement test scores of 11 to 17 percent.[51]

This finding came from a review of 317 studies, which involved 324,303 kids. The studies found several other positive impacts, such as a better connection to school, increased prosocial behavior, and a reduction in student conduct problems. And, to put a cherry on top, the findings were found to be applicable for racially and ethnically diverse students from urban, rural, and suburban settings.

Extending these findings, we would suggest that putting people in the position of their own expertise, as this section describes, may even help to build up the identity in someone who says, "I am smart. I am capable. I have something to offer." That is a mindset that goes beyond increasing test scores. It creates changemakers.

I often get hung up on being right, and it is hard for me to know the other person is also right. However, they are. They are right in how they see the world, regardless of my own convictions. It can be hard to follow my curiosity in those moments. However, I have often asked myself, "How does that worldview get created?" or "How did they create that worldview?" when someone does something that is outside of how I see the world. For instance, when I hear about suicide bombers I often wonder, "How does that happen?" How do they feel so strongly about something that they are willing to give their lives (and take others' lives) for it? I will never be able to have that conversation with anyone (on this planet, anyway), for they will already be gone by the time they live their convictions to the fullest extent possible. Nevertheless, how interesting would it be to discover how they see the world and to really listen? How much would my world be expanded by the process? It would be easy for me to see that they are wrong. It would be more fruitful for me to challenge my own worldview by remembering that they think they are right and see it as an opportunity for discovery. Even if my intention or desire is to fix a broken person, I will have much more success if I can fully discover the brokenness first.

Closer to home, one of my students was a victim of a hate crime. He was called some nasty names and hit over the head with a bottle while he was leaving his apartment. I feel for him. His life is forever, majorly changed as a result of the physical and mental injuries. My first response toward the attackers is anger. However, if I can pause and think about them, I can find that place where I feel for them as well.

I would love to sit with them and discover how it is that they see the world. How do they feel so strongly about something— very different from the things for which I feel strongly—that they are willing to do violence against someone?

Judgment and empathy live in two different houses. Living in judgment rarely allows me to learn or see anything new. If I want to leave the house of judgment, a place I can go is the house of empathy, and curiosity will be what gets me there, even when I disagree with what I see when I arrive.

▶ Tool: Ask so that they describe their world

Once you have reflected back what you understand about their worldview, you might ask an empathic question. Ask a question that helps both of you describe the world as they see it.

Asking empathic questions can be quite difficult (this is where the art is). Practice is key. One way to begin that practice is to ask questions that allow the other person to tell you more about how they see the world from their own perspective. At this point, you are not trying to lead them anywhere. You are only asking, "Where are you on this map of yours?" and maybe, "Where are you going on this map?" or even more simply, "Show me your map; how was it created?"

Questions can often be asked from an empathic place if they address what the other person fears, what they aspire to, what their history is, or how what is happening now fits into the bigger picture of who they are. If you can clearly see the story they are telling themselves about who they are in the world, you are on the right path. Your job is to help them capture how they see the world, how the world impacts them, and all that they believe to be true. Suddenly, you have become a coauthor to their autobiography.

Imagine someone calls into a customer service center:

CALLER "I'm eighty-seven years old and I'm having a difficult time using my computer."

CUSTOMER SERVICE REPRESENTATIVE "Go to our website and watch the how-to videos."

Can you imagine the response of the caller? They were just told to do more of the thing they cannot do. How often do we listen to our friends, family, and coworkers in this way? We offer something that was helpful for *us* at some point but do not make a point to listen to what the other's needs are. We dismiss their fear, because it was unfounded (at least from our own perspective), and we don't hear what is really going on for them. We can rarely offer anything helpful if we don't have an understanding of where they are in *this* moment.

How would the conversation be different if the customer service representative took a moment to really understand—empathically understand—the caller's comfort level with technology?

CALLER "I'm eighty-seven years old and I'm having a difficult time using my computer."

CUSTOMER SERVICE REPRESENTATIVE "You are feeling lost and unsure what to do."

CALLER "Yes, exactly, and I need help so I can email my grandson who's in the Peace Corps."

CUSTOMER SERVICE REPRESENTATIVE "Sounds like communicating with him is important. Let's see if we can discover what the problem is. What are you having a difficult time with?"

A scripted response will not work. The customer service representative cannot respond to each caller with the same language and simultaneously be empathic. Being empathic requires the representative to be open to the caller and respond to them in a unique way—a way that is particular for who the person is in that specific moment.

▶ **Trap: How does that make you feel?**

When people are learning to respond to others in an empathic way, they often begin to sound like a therapist and ask, "How does that make you feel?" This is potentially a useful question, and it is also very limited. It narrows the possible reaction to an experience based only on feelings. Moreover, if people feel like you are practicing pop psychology, they often clam up (see Chapter 3 on Openness).

Instead of asking, "How does that make you feel?" try questions like:

▸ What is it like for you to experience . . . ?
▸ What struck you?
▸ What was that like for you?
▸ What was your response?

▶ **Tool: Use other senses to listen**

Listen with your ears, eyes, heart, smell, and touch.

Deep listening requires you to listen with all of yourself. It requires you to stay present to what is happening as best you can. There are no "time outs" to get your argument together or to daydream about what they are saying and how it fits into your own life. (If you are creating a response in your head, you are not listening to what is being said in that moment.) It is simply listening. Deep listening.

Listening with Your Eyes

In my early twenties, while teaching in an outdoor setting, I was impressed with my own ability to read minds. One of the boys was standing before me trying to listen but squirming in his pants. I told him he could run behind a big tree and go pee. He flew off like a shot. None of the other kids was impressed with my ability to read his mind. I was shocked by this, and was for many years. To me, it felt like a magic trick. Why was no one else impressed? Now that I'm a parent, I can see this skill is one that every parent quickly learns, and young children seem to expect adults to know how full their bladder is at all times. I impressed myself then because I employed the tactic of listening—not with my ears, but with my eyes. It is not really all that impressive. We do it all the time.

One way to listen with all of yourself is to listen with each of your senses. Lots of good listening happens with your eyes. Watching what they do with their body is a huge clue about who they are in the world.

Watching another person's body language is natural and part

of who we are. If you watch small children, even those under two, you can see how they begin to match the body language of those close to them. Somehow, as we grow up, we forget to pay attention. Relearning to listen with your eyes might require you to engage your brain. Some questions to ask yourself when you're trying to listen with your eyes are:

- How does what this person is saying (with words) match what their body is doing?
- How does what this person is saying not match what their body is doing?

One note here: The body can be a direct translation of the heart and mind, but it is silly to suggest that we will know exactly what someone is feeling or thinking based on body language alone. However, we can allow it to add to what we ask of others.

Often, we are making an assumption when we read body language. Making assumptions can get you into trouble. However, taking your assumption and turning it into a question is a great way to explore whether you and the other person are on the same page. Once confirmed, you can ask a powerful question that will explore new territory rather than move forward on false assumptions.

A powerful question can almost always be discovered if you notice incongruence between someone's body language and his or her words. If they are saying one thing, but their body language isn't aligned with their words, then gently ask a question that explores that difference. I say "gently" because it is a risky place to go, and it's easy to create a situation in which they feel they need to defend themselves (as the example below would suggest).

That is why the "People-watching/People-being" exercise in the self-work section is so powerful. It helps you develop a skill in which you have a deeper understanding of where others might be.

For instance, you notice that Maria is sitting in a confined and limited way. Both her arms and legs are close to her body with very little movement. Her spine is rounded forward with the shoulders crunched. This is different from what you normally notice about her; she normally speaks with her hands and has a more open stance. Her words, however, don't seem to match her limited posture. She is saying, "Mom and I have a special relationship that is open. We tell each other everything that is going on. I know what is going on before her best friends know what is happening. We are best friends."

In your mind, these words do not match what you see. You make an assumption that either her mom is keeping something from her or she is afraid to tell her mom something.

So what do you do?

I recommend NOT saying the following if you want to avoid the world of judging:

- ▸ I don't believe you.
- ▸ Your words don't match your body.
- ▸ I notice that you are closed off as you say that.

Sometimes the statements above will work to open the conversation further, especially if you have really good rapport. However, they are mostly limited responses.

It is best to be more exploratory—be a stranger in a new land where things don't make sense. Ask questions to get a lay of the land. Allow them to be an expert in what they know to be true and let them express that to you. You have a clue that something is amiss and you can use it but not as a sword that cuts deep. Your opportunity is more like a detective's magnifying glass, a place to focus. Give them the opportunity to share their view of what they think isn't lining up and why.

So, what DO you do? Questions you might ask:

▸ What is going on right now with your mom?
▸ What has your mom taught you about being yourself?
▸ How did your mom foster such an open relationship with you?
▸ What experiences have you had with your mom lately?

You could use reflective statements like:

▸ You are best friends. *(Verbatim.)*
▸ Sounds like being open with your mom is important to you. *(Verbatim and Simple Translation.)*
▸ Being real and open with mom is your normal. *(Simple Translation that allows them to say that something is not normal at present.)*

- Your relationship with your mom is unique and something is not right about it right now. *(Far Out that allows her to say more about what, if anything, is wrong.)*
- You value your relationship with your mom and being best friends with her. You have told me stories before about how she has been keeping secrets—like that time you told me about her dating website profile and that you did not know about it. *(Connecting the Dots opens the door to see if this time is like what happened before.)*

What you have done here is pointed to a moment and said, "I want to explore this piece before we go on, for something is a bit curious here," without actually coming right out and saying it. The challenge here is not to judge (or sound judgmental) because their body language does not match their words but to be curious about the story behind the inconsistent language. It is a way to go deeper into what is real for them and to explore something that may not even have occurred to them yet.

Listening with Your Other Senses

Some people say that real listening happens with your eyes. We have explored that in relationship to body language. Now, we will explore what your other senses might tell you. Can real listening happen with your nose? How about your skin? Maybe even your taste buds? (Okay, that one might be really weird.) Let me give a few examples of what I'm talking about.

Once, I was facilitating a group on the topic of race. A member of the group was having a difficult time engaging and always seemed to be a bit off-topic or a bit late in the conversation. When he spoke, his eyes seemed to take a moment to focus on those he was talking to and would roll away soon after initial eye contact. I was confused about how to address this, so I paused and took a deep breath, trying to decide how to proceed. It was then I noticed the smell: lots of alcohol coming through his skin. I don't think he was drunk in that moment, but I think he had drunk enough the day before that it made it difficult for him to be present with the group.

It was hard for me to be empathic that day—really hard, actually, because I don't drink. I have been sick with a headache to the point where bright light and loud noises were not welcomed events, but never as the result of a hangover. I also had a sense that this was not a first-time event for him because the group had already had difficulty with him in the past.

Therefore, I decided when he was off-topic or delayed that it was best for me to affirm him, usually with reflective listening. I kept the group conversation moving forward by quickly following the reflection with a question to the group. I also decided to keep my eyes open for a moment to explore his impact on the group. Sometime later, he said something that was so off-base that a few group members looked at me like, "Are you going to really let that slide?" So I said, "Luke, let's leave this topic for just a second and talk about you. What is making it difficult for you to be present with this group?" He apologized and said he was trying and that he did not feel good.

The group laughed, and some people said, "We know." He got the message. We moved back to the topic, he was more authentic later (rather than faking it), and he said how he appreciated the group and promised to be more present next time.

So, did I listen with my nose? My nose definitely informed me of his current state. Deep listening requires listening with our whole selves. All of the senses are tuned in to what is present in this moment. It might be funny to say that listening can happen with anything but the ears, and yet the great listeners I know have a way of listening with their whole body. They are completely invested in what is present with no distractions. They are able to suspend judgment and hear what is present as it is.

When you listen with your whole self, you become aware of aspects of the conversation that have always been there, but you may not have been able to be fully aware of them. On the other hand, maybe you've have had some awareness but weren't quite able to pinpoint exactly what was "missing."

Once you listen with your whole self, you will be able to access parts of the conversation that are almost inaccessible, unless you are listening with your whole self. This can have a huge positive impact on how the dialogue moves forward and how people contribute. Remember, people want to be heard. Listening with your whole self allows you to have access to dealing with the part of the conversation that is sometime called resistance, defiance, contempt, or even backtalk. This might be someone not willing to share or someone having an emotional response they feel like they can't control.

I was once asked to facilitate a retreat for a leadership team of twelve people for the largest organization of its kind in the nation. The CEO was new to the organization and asked me to help her leadership team deal with some huge obstacles that she saw on the horizon. Early in the morning, after getting connected and sharing a few laughs, I asked everyone to sit in a circle with no desks or tables. After I gave an overview of the day, shared some ground rules, invited people to fully participate, and dealt with some logistics, we started moving forward in our first important dialogue.

My first question was, "What would it require from each of us to be in full trust with each other?" A few people started sharing answers that were moving us forward in understanding. One woman was of particular interest to me. She had not spoken to the whole group yet and she was sitting with her arms crossed, her hands in fists, and her feet planted flat on the floor as if she was prepared to fight. When others spoke, she sighed heavily or rolled her eyes. When the CEO shared her vision, the muscles on this woman's arms and face flexed. Whatever was going on for her, it appeared to me as resistance, and it needed to come into the room in order for us to fully experience a conversation around trust. There had to be room for her in this conversation, even if she was cynical about what was happening. Finally, I took advantage of a lull in conversation and invited her to share by looking at her and smiling. Off she went! To paraphrase: "I don't understand why we're here. We didn't get an agenda, you've been using lots of jargon, and now we're talking about trust. What did we do wrong?"

I could have seen this as a personal attack. Instead, I smiled. I quickly thought through the points she was making in her attack.

- ▸ I wasn't sure why the CEO hadn't shared an agenda.
- ▸ I was not aware of any jargon that I used (other than maybe "lean into the fear").
- ▸ Trust is foundational to an effective leadership team.

I could have easily been tempted to push upon that resistance. Instead, I used some of the tools below to invite her into the conversation. I reflected, "You're unsure why you are here?" As the conversation continued, she became pivotal in helping the group really explore what trust would look like for them. When the resistance is held and accepted, rather than pushed or ignored, something magical can happen. Often, we deal with this resistance by pushing back harder or completely ignoring it.

What is one crucial ingredient for true happiness?

What are you grateful for?

▶ Trap: Pushing upon the resistance

If you find that you are pushing on the resistance, it might be an indicator that you are not being empathic and that you are thinking about your own needs and desires. Pushing might look like throwing blame on the person who is expressing resistance, telling them what they need to do (as in giving them a directive), or it might be trying to tell them they are wrong. Conveying your own perspective has become more important than clearly seeing the perspective of the other. Often what happens when you push is that the other begins to push harder. That might look like a raised voice, justifying their stance, or repeating themselves because they assume you aren't clear on what they're saying. Most of us attempt to counteract this greater resistance when we sense it. This pushback turns into a cycle in which the power of wills between facilitator and the speaker become the most important task at hand.

▶ Antidote: Find the resistance and let it be named

Rather than standing defiant against the resistance you encounter, step aside and allow the full force of the resistance to be present, but not pushing upon you. Like an Aikido master, who takes a small step to allow an attacker to fall to his feet rather than pushing with an equal force back. Find a way in which the resistance can be named, can be seen, and usually it will dissolve (e.g., "You are unsure why you are here" or "You are wondering if you did something wrong"). One way to do this effectively in conversation is to understand the difference between content and process.

▶ Tool: Leave content and go to process

Another way to use empathy in forming a question is to leave the **Content** (what you are talking about) completely and go to a place that we call **Process** (how you are talking about it).

In thinking about a conversation, making choices about how to proceed, and asking your next powerful question, there are two parts to consider:

- **Content** may be the most obvious and where we spend the majority of our effort when trying to form the next powerful question. Content is the words we are actually using. It is the subject matter or the *what* you are talking about.

- **Process**, on the other hand, is *how* you are talking about the content. It could be said that process is all other communication besides the words being used.

CONTENT *What* We Are Talking About	PROCESS *How* We Are Talking About the Content
The words	**Examples include:**
The subject	Lecture
The topic	Dialogue
The themes	Speaking with excitement or monotone
	Listening to win like in a debate
	ALL other communication while we talk about the thing we are talking about (body language, tone, inflection, rhythm, silence, who we are being)

Let's look at part of a conversation as an example:

JOSE "I don't understand how Americans have forgotten so quickly that they live in a country that was all immigrants, except for the few Native Americans. It frustrates me that Americans can support stupid immigration laws."

SALLY "Don't you understand that we are not what we once were? There are no jobs left for the people who currently live here. How can we allow more to come in if we can't employ the ones who are here? It is really an issue of overpopulation worldwide."

What is the content?

CONTENT *What* We Are Talking About	PROCESS *How* We Are Talking About the Content
American history	
Current immigration laws	
Unemployment	
Not understanding	
Overpopulation	

What is the process? That is harder to understand with the example as it has been given, so far. It needs some more detail, much in the same way a play might show notes for the actors. So, let's try that.

JOSE *(His face is getting red, he spits and crosses his arms.)* "I don't understand how Americans have forgotten so quickly that they live in a country that was all immigrants *(he is raising his voice)*, except for the few Native Americans *(suddenly he is speaking softer)*. It frustrates me that Americans can support stupid immigration laws."

SALLY *(Raising her voice, yet is almost pleading as she changes the subject.)* "Don't you understand that we are not what we once were? There are no jobs left for the people who currently live here *(shifting her body so she is looking away from him)*. How can we allow more to come in if we can't employ the ones who are here? It is really an issue of overpopulation worldwide."

Now can we describe the process? Here we are going to create a list of process moments alongside the content to represent how content and process are happening at the same time. The process may be a result of the words being said or, more often, they may be a reaction to other process moments in the room. The content and process may or may not be related to each other.

CONTENT *What* We Are Talking About	PROCESS *How* We Are Talking About the Content
American history	Red-faced
Current immigration laws	Raised voice
Unemployment	Spitting, crossing arms
Not understanding	Raised voice, pleading in response to him crossing his arms
Unemployment	Shifting body, looking away from Jose
Overpopulation	Changing the subject

All the things now listed under **Process**, plus many more not listed, are subtle bits of communication that are contributing to the conversation in some way. Each of these cues is communicating something to the other person, and that person is responding in some way.

Process can be really broad, too. Are we talking about a subject in a lecture format or face to face with equal exchange on each side? Are we sitting so our shoulders are squared, facing each other, or side-by-side as if on a park bench?

▶ Tool: Ask a process question

Anytime the content is not working for everyone involved, leave it for a moment. You can almost always ask a powerful question or provide a reflective statement, from the place of process. Leave the content, and ask some questions about *how* you are talking about the content. Who are they being while they are talking about that *what*? This will usually catch people off guard for a minute, but it will give you something meaningful, especially if you can do it in a way that does not create defensiveness. It is equally useful to do this in a group setting or one-on-one. The way that you leave the content and go to process is the same individually and in groups.

If you were observing the above example with Jose and Sally, you could say:

> "It's obvious that you both feel strongly about something here. Where did these views come from?" *(Mild process question with some content.)*

"Wait a moment. Let's leave this topic for just a moment and let's talk about what has us so worked up right now." *(Wholly process.)*

"Hold on a second. Let's pause! What is making it hard to listen right now?" *(Wholly process and risky—it would be easy for them to say, "I am listening, and she is nuts.")*

If it were just Sally and Jose talking, Sally could say:

"Jose, I want to talk about this some more after I understand what got you so worked up. What makes you feel the need to spit for emphasis?" *(Mild process question that may provide an understanding of the content—history of immigration laws in the US—or more process—family member got arrested for working illegally.)*

Sally says, "Jose, hold on a moment. What is really going on?" Jose says, "What do you mean?" Sally, "Come on, Jose, you just spit. You only do that when you are really angry. What really happened to get you so worked up?" *(Wholly process.)*

Jose could influence the conversation by moving to process by asking:

"Sally, hold on a sec. We could talk about population dynamics if you want to, but it seems like there is something going on for you right now. What has happened that you are feeling so strongly about employment rates?"

▶ Trap: "But I can't stop the conversation"

Yes, this requires pausing the conversation (content) and addressing something (process) that is influencing the conversation but is not being talked about. That "something" might be resistance. It might be any number of things. Often my students get very worried about stopping a conversation, especially one that has gotten heated and intense or one that gets people worked up. Moreover, some facilitators actually get excited when things become emotionally intense: "Now we are getting somewhere!" However, if it's really hot, then more often than not, few are really listening—or if they are, they are listening to win or listening to get their ideas across. "Heated" usually means that listening to understand is no longer present, no longer possible, and that participants have become so worked up or invested in the content that they do not see what impact all the other forms of communication (process) are having on the conversation. If you ignore this, then you are ignoring the humans sitting with you. The process part of the conversation is *them*. Asking questions from a place of process acknowledges that you see them. It will make the conversation more impactful. People might be able to really listen to others in a way that they could not before because you have just humanized everyone.

How enriching would this conversation be if you could get both Sally and Jose to share why their views about immigration are so strong? What if they learn they both have a story about their fathers that is the same and different? (He is sad because his father is getting deported, and she is sad because hers is losing a job.) From this place, they would be able to see the story from the other side, in a more humanizing way, and there would be more empathy in the room as a whole.

▶ **Tool: Give yourself permission to pause the conversation**

When do you pause a conversation and go to process? The first rule is experience. Learn from both failure and success to gain experience.

That may not be very helpful right now, so here are two guidelines to help you as you gain experience. I'm calling them "rules," although they are perhaps better explained as "rules of thumb." Use them to help guide you, and give yourself permission to leave the content of the conversation to dig into what might be influencing the conversation by exploring the process. The two rules are called "Rule of Three" and "The Big One."

The Rule of Three

When you're in a conversation, you can use the Rule of Three to explore whether there is something unknown to you that is influencing the conversation.

Simply stated: The Rule of Three is useful when there are three interruptions in the content of the conversation which you can clearly identify (without judgment), coming from some unknown emotional response. When this occurs, pause the conversation and ask about the process. In other words, choose connection rather than content.

> You are about to have a conversation with your usually timely boss, Heather, about an idea you are excited about. You walk into her office at the agreed time.

> **YOU** "Hey, Boss, thanks for agreeing to meet with me to explore the possibility about . . ."

HEATHER "Hold on!" She never looks up from her computer. "I need about five more minutes."

YOU "Okay, Boss." You sit outside her office and wait. After about eight minutes, you hear . . .

HEATHER "Okay, come on in. What is it that you want to talk about?"

YOU "Thanks. We are here to talk about this new possibility for improving customer relationships." *(Being clear about the intent.)*

HEATHER "Oh, right, you have a harebrained scheme that will make customers fly in the door." *(Oh, yes, that was sarcasm.)*

YOU "I don't know if they will fly in, but they will be more connected . . ."

HEATHER "Hold on!" Picks up the phone and makes a call.

YOU "Sure."

HEATHER Hangs up the phone and says, "Sorry, I had to do that before I forgot."

YOU "No worries."

HEATHER "What were you saying?"

YOU "Improving customer relations is important as we move into this next phase of . . ." You stop talking as you see Heather looking everywhere as if she has misplaced something.

HEATHER "Keep going! I need to find my pen to take some notes."

YOU "There is one right there in your pen cup."

HEATHER "Not that one, I got this new one I'm excited about. It floats across the page. You should get one."

How many times did Heather do something that might suggest she is not invested in the conversation? Count them.

What do you do now?

1. Do you plow ahead? *(This generally gets you a bunch of wasted time.)*
2. Do you call her out on it? "You don't care about this idea, do you?" *(Potentially detrimental to your employment.)*
3. Do you do something else?

If you can identify the moments that she was pulled from the conversation (observing without judgment), then you might try your luck at using the Rule of Three. Let's see how many moments you can identify. It is best not to name things that are done "wrong" but purely things you can see, without the filter of what they might mean. It may be tempting to pass judgment on Heather's actions, so I have included what those judgments might look like in the following chart. I have listed more than three to make the examples clear, but you only need three to use this tool effectively.

Heather did the following:

Observation	Turned into Judgment
She needed to start later than planned.	She does not have time to meet with me. (It appears that is the case, but you are jumping to judgment.)
She asked for five more minutes but needed eight.	She is stressed.
She never greeted me or looked up to make eye contact.	She does not care about me.
She used sarcasm.	She does not like my idea and thinks it is childish.
She made a phone call during our meeting.	She has more important things to do than talk to me. She does not care about me.
She forgot what I was talking about.	She does not like this idea.
She is looking for something.	Whatever she is looking for is more important than I am. She is not listening.
She changes the subject (to her new pen).	"Pens are more important than our customers! You dumb jerk."

How quickly we jump from observation (something we can see and/or hear) to making a judgment about it.

To use the Rule of Three well, especially from the place of empathy, one needs to clearly state what you observe (as purely an observation). One way to think about doing this is how you would draw what you see: the large hand of a clock eight minutes past the top of the hour or someone looking for a pen. To make an observation, more description is sometimes necessary to stave off judgment.

In this example, you have more than three indicators of some kind of emotional response that is affecting the conversation. After three clear observations that there is some kind of emotional response, you have an open invite to leave the content and explore what it might be that is distracting from the conversation at hand.

You also have one big problem. You and your boss never connected. Ideas do not really get shared (and especially are never built upon) with people unless they are connected. Ideas might get stolen, they might get killed, but they will not get planted and grow unless people are connected.

How often have you seen or been part of a dynamic like this in the workplace? You could leave this meeting thinking that your boss is a jerk and that you have lots of data to support this.

One way to connect with your boss is to pause the content, name your observations, and ask about them.

> **YOU** "Heather, may I pause this conversation before we go any further? Since I walked into your office, you started this meeting late, you've made a phone call, and now we are talking about pens. What is going on?" (Notice you did not say: "Heather, it is obvious that you don't have time for my idea. I'm leaving.")

Then you wait. Just wait in silence. Let the situation be as it is and don't try to fix it, make it better, or make it go away. Wait, make eye contact, and be ready to listen. The answer will often surprise you. The other person might be shocked that you have pointed out their lack of presence in the conversation so clearly without any judgment. Handled with judgment applied, their natural inclination might be to defend or to attack you back. However, when you have stated your observation with no judgment, there is little need for them to feel defensive, and there is nothing to attack. It is as if you held a mirror up to their actions and they can see how they have not been present (or present to something else more important for them).

HEATHER "Oh, it's true, something else is going on. I cannot talk about it much, but my boss is not happy with some numbers that I have given him and I feel like I'm in the hot seat."

YOU "That sounds like a difficult place to be. How do you want to proceed?" (It is important to give the other person a choice about how to move forward, because you are not going to be productive anyway unless they are fully engaged. Moreover, don't give them a way out by trying to fix the situation for them: e.g., "Would you like to reschedule or cancel or . . .")

HEATHER "Do you think your idea will help with the bottom line?" *(She is moving back to content. Sometimes you might need to listen for a while before moving the conversation back to content.)*

YOU "I know it will."

HEATHER "Then let's proceed, and I will be a better listener. It could be the best thing that happens all day. What's your idea?" *(She can now choose to be connected and engaged, whereas before, she was a prisoner of her emotions and did not know it.)*

You can also leave the content and go to process in the middle of a conversation—or anytime, for that matter. For instance, "Can I pause you for a moment? Since we began talking about this, you have gone silent, pulled your chair back, and checked your watch several times. What is going on?"

Once they have shared, you may find it useful to reflect what you heard. Give them some choice about how to proceed (without trying to fix it for them or be the "therapist"). It is important for them to choose so they can be fully present. If you choose for them or attempt to fix the situation for them, they will often stay right where they are. When appropriate, bring the conversation back to content (usually within a moment or two).

The Rule of Three in short:
Leave content when you see three actions that might be indicators that something is interrupting the conversation.

- ▸ Pause the conversation.
- ▸ State what actions you've observed (without judgment)— things that may be pointing to an emotional response.
- ▸ Quickly follow up by asking something like, "What is going on?" and wait in silence.

- Once the other person responds, give a Reflective Listening Statement or ask, "Is there any more you need/want to say?"
- When they are finished speaking, ask, "How do you want to proceed?" Make sure they have some choice in the matter.
- Return to content, if appropriate.

The Big One

There will be times when you will not need to wait until you get three observations. In rare cases, all you need to do is count to one, but the one is so BIG that you get it immediately. It will often be shocking and is best if tended to right away.

There are many ways in which this could appear. Here are just a few to give you an idea:

- shouted profanities coming from someone who does not normally swear
- slamming a fist on a table
- walking or storming out of the room

The steps are the same as in the Rule of Three:

1. Name what you see without judgment. ("You are hitting the table," not "You're so angry you're not even listening.")
2. Ask about it. ("What is going on for you right now?")
3. Wait for a response, in silence, with eye contact and while maintaining openness inside yourself
4. Listen, and reflect if needed. ("You are coming up against a tough place, and you don't know what to do.")

5. Ask how they want to proceed. ("Thanks for sharing. How would you like to proceed now?")
6. Direct them back to the topic. ("Okay, we were sharing how this might impact . . .")

If The Big One appears, you have enough data to leave the content as soon as possible and go directly to process to see what is influencing the conversation. This is a tool in your toolbox that you will rarely use, and when it is time to use it, it will be the perfect tool.

Both The Big One and the Rule of Three give you ways to access the part of the conversation (process) that seemed unavailable before. I'm suggesting that the process should be accessed anytime it could have a positive impact on the conversation. In the world of process, we are communicating loads of stuff that people are seeing as truth and that is not being verbalized. In having the wisdom to call forth what you are observing as pure observation, everyone can get a handle on what is really going on. As a result, everyone can choose to step into a world in which empathy is present, rather than apathy.

Did you know?

Empathy is contagious, and it can promote cooperation. Researchers at the University of Pennsylvania concluded this after recent behavioral analyses.[52]

We became curious about which empathetic behaviors could really become contagious in groups. We stumbled on a fascinating study on data from 87,000 360-degree feedback assessments. The research was trying to break down the core ingredients of trust. The study uncovered that the number one element of trust was positive relationships. "Woo-hoo," we thought. This was quickly followed by a "Duh!" This was not particularly surprising *until* they went on to break down how top leaders build "positive relationships." Here are several core actions a leader must take to build positive, trusting relationships:

1. Stay in touch on the issues and concerns **of others**.

2. Balance results with concern **for others**.

3. Generate cooperation **between others**.

4. Resolve conflict **with others**.

Of others. For others. Between others. And ultimately "with others." The common element involves "others." At the final level of the Asking Powerful Questions Pyramid™, we use the words "with you" to capture empathy. We chose these words because when you communicate from a mindset of "I am with you," your intentions, curiosities, listening, and reflections are all received so much more positively. When we experience true empathy, it feels like the other person is on our team and has our best interest in mind. Like they are *with you*.

As you consider the tips below on how empathy can be applied in groups, consider that your empathy as a leader can be contagious. Learn more at www.weand.me/empathy.

How Empathy Can Be Applied in Groups

The Rule of Three and The Big One are useful in a large group, as well as one-on-one. For example, let's say you are in a board meeting and you are talking about a new initiative that you believe will have a better impact on the customers than the current model. As you are talking, one person checks their phone, another looks out the window, and another asks you questions about an unrelated topic.

In these moments, a natural response is to plow through and get the work done (or attempt to, anyway). In my case, plowing though often looks like talking faster, louder, or more animatedly. My hands start talking, too, as if things will get done if I wave them around as much as possible. Whatever resistance is present I push hard against to move in the "correct" direction. However, I don't get any real work done in these moments, for the group is not connected. Something unbeknownst to me has come between us. I see the actions of those I'm with telling me there is something between us, in the same way I can see the ripples on a smooth lake when the water has been disturbed. Often, I jump to assumptions and suddenly "know" what has created the ripples. "Ah, a rock has been thrown in" or "They are nervous about what their boss is going to think about this." Yet, in reality, I know nothing. I'm only guessing and, as a result, have placed one more thing between us—my assumption about what is going on for them. If I take a step toward connection, rather than continue my own judgment of the situation, the whole conversation can shift.

By using the Rule of Three, everyone has been invited to play a different game. A game of realness. I draw a line and state with my words and actions something like, "What we've been doing up to this point has been on the surface. I want to see all of you. Who is really here with me and what is going on?" The odd thing is that I sometimes opt not to take this step because I'm afraid it will take more time. The reality is that most often it takes far *less* time than neglecting to connect. As soon as people are seen, and we move toward connection, the junk that is in the space between us gets cleared, and in that space fully engaged humans show up, ready to make a difference.

The Rule of Three allows you to look at people's emotional responses that are showing up in the room and yet invisible. In making them visible, you are creating an atmosphere that says, "Being fake is not worth our time; being real is." If you have stated that you value the people you work with, your authentic self has just arrived. This authenticity invites others to move toward authenticity. Finally, you are communicating that you don't want to waste your time or anyone else's.

It takes courage to stop plowing the infertile soil during a lifeless meeting (for you feel like you are doing *something*) and move toward connection. Take a breath and leave the content for a moment to ask about what is really going on. You might say, "Seems like I might be missing something. Since we have started, I see people checking their phones, looking out the window, and asking questions about other topics. What is going on that I'm missing?"

They now know that you see them and you are making a step toward connection. You have made your intention clear and have invited others into an empathic space. Your job then will be to be a silent listener, and you might be surprised. Once you understand where people's emotional responses are coming from, ask them how they want to proceed. You can then direct them back to the content, if appropriate, once the emotional response has been revealed.

Summary of Empathy

I have given you several models in this section, intended to help you move more easily in the realm of empathy. From a place of empathy, we can ask truly powerful questions.

When you notice you are asking questions that are only chasing after facts, go to a place that seeks deeper understanding.

When you notice you are asking questions that are heavily in the *feeling* department, what are you missing? People are more than just what they feel. You are missing their whole story—what they fear, what they aspire to, how they see the world. You are missing the story of how they got to this moment (background), or you are missing the story of who they are—and the stories they believe about who they are! If you are noticing that your story is becoming the focus of your thoughts or words ("That reminds me of the time . . ."), you have lost their story. Ask questions so that their story becomes the focus.

When you are having a difficult time being empathic, a place to start is simply to describe the world as they see it. "It sounds like you believe . . ."

If the content of conversation is not working for whatever reason, you can often go to process to explore what is really happening.

Use the Rule of Three anytime you need to give yourself permission to interrupt and look at process or a hidden emotional response.

Self-Work for Empathy

People-Watching, People-Being

One way to practice this is to go to a public place and watch people from a distance. As you are watching someone, try to understand what is going through their heart and head. Then place yourself in that same position. If they are sitting with crossed legs and leaning forward with shoulders slightly crunched, then you try to place yourself in a similar position. What do you notice about your own thoughts and feelings? Does anything surprise you? If the space allows, after the person leaves, try going to the same spot and placing yourself in the position you saw them in. Even shift your body weight to the same side they had it. Now look where they were looking. Notice your thoughts and feelings. You will never know (unless you ask to confirm) what is truly going through their heart and mind, but

this activity allows you to sharpen your knowledge of what their body language might mean. When you increase your ability to read the body language of others, you can use that information to inform your powerful questions. Experience it for yourself and see what occurs for you.

We!

With you	EMPATHY
I get you	LISTENING
I hear you	OPENNESS
I see you	RAPPORT
I am willing to know you	INTENTION

Chapter 6

Advanced Skills

This chapter offers six additional skills that will support you in moving into the *art* of asking powerful questions. I recommend cultivating these skills after you have practiced Intention, Rapport, Openness, Listening, and Empathy. You will find that the Pyramid will support you as you work on these skills.

- *Debate and Dialogue:* What distinguishes Debate from Dialogue, and how to expertly move between the two as needed.
- *Silence:* How to use silence for the benefit of all.
- *Web-Building:* How to build connections between people in a group setting.
- *Defining Words:* A trap that often shows up when people spend too much time defining the words they are using.
- *Overtalking:* What to do when someone is dominating the group conversation.
- *Steering into the Curve:* How to face the difficult moments.
- *Working with Co-Facilitators:* Tools to lead with another facilitator.

Debate and Dialogue

Don't Make Assumptions.
Find the courage to ask questions and
express what you really want.

— Don Miguel Ruiz[53] —

This tool delves into what dialogue is and how it is different from debate. We will also examine how you can move a conversation from where people see each other as "someone to defeat" to a place in which all at the table are seen as equals.

Distinguishing debate and dialogue is another model to understand where conversations might go and what you can do to manage them, as a facilitator, so that you are able to generate powerful questions that are the most useful to the moment.

When participants walk in the room and you are doing your best to establish rapport, most often the group will be at the place called casual conversation. In order to get the conversation to move to a place of *dialogue*, you can use all the tools given to you in this book, creating a space where people can choose to trust and take risks. Don't forget to clearly state your intention in being together.

How will you know that the group is in **dialogue**? Here are some indicators you can explore:

- ▸ People are listening for understanding.
- ▸ There are multiple perspectives being shared (often with no clear answers).

- You are hearing personal stories or reflections (if appropriate to intention or group's goals).
- People are open and reflective to what is being said in the room.
- People are seeing others as equals and are open to their humanity.
- People are able to be empathic.

Sometimes, the conversation can move from dialogue to debate. The following list might help you discern when the conversation turned into **debate**:

- People are listening for (and responding to) the flaw in what the other person is saying.
- There are usually only two perspectives in the room. The issue has become polarized.
- Sometimes people are sharing facts or statistics to prove their point.
- People only want to WIN and prove their point (and are not open or reflective). Convincing, selling, or persuading may be present.
- Usually, they do not see their fellow participants as equals but as opponents to be defeated.
- People are focused on themselves and do not consider others.
- There is a feeling of argument in the room. Someone might be offended.

So, how did you get from a place of dialogue to debate? There are a number of small actions that potentially contribute to this dynamic.

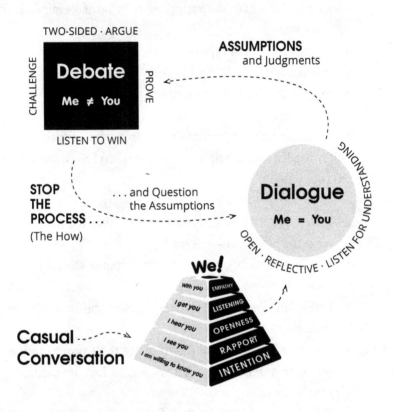

One way is that you asked a leading question to which you expected a specific outcome or answer. For example, "What is the right choice, then?" Some of the group's members, sensing this push, resist it, and suddenly two camps are in the room. Perhaps you created a situation in which the people who are competitive feel the need to win. For example, "Who can tell us the correct answer to our problem?"

In some cases, someone's trigger might have been activated. When this happens, there is a strong emotional response in the room and a sense that there's a great injustice that needs to be fixed. It might be your own trigger, or it might be one of the other participant's. For example, I recently heard a woman loudly say, "I should be able to wear what I want to wear, when I want to wear it, without fearing how men are going to respond!" She moved to the edge of her seat and began to stare down the woman who was speaking before her (whose words she'd cut off). Soon, the conversation was a full-blown debate, with people taking a firm stand and unable to hear a different viewpoint from their own. Anyone who didn't share their view was wrong.

How did we get to debate so quickly? It is true that someone's need to win has appeared, or someone's trigger might have been hit. When we look more closely, there is almost always something that is influencing the conversation that seems elusive or invisible. If you can find it, you can steer the conversation in a more productive direction. The path from dialogue to debate is often filled with assumptions and judgment. Somewhere, there is an assumption in the room that is influencing the dynamic. Directly connected to that assumption is judgment. This assumption is now influencing the way people are seeing each other, leading to judgments about each other's level of intelligence that prevents them from fully seeing each other. Each one is now only looking for the fatal flaw in what others are saying and opportunities to prove they are wrong. The *What* you are talking about (content) has become more important than the *How* you are talking about it (process). The assumptions and judgments beget more assumption and judgment, encouraging challenges and attacks.

Let me be clear: I am not saying that debate is bad. It might be useful for the group, actually. Oftentimes when a debate is instigated, there is more energy and people are more engaged. Being in that space for a limited time can be useful. However, it is important to note that it creates a dynamic in the room in which multiple perspectives are not allowed to be present. Do complex issues really only have two sides, as appears to be the case during a debate? This will affect your group outcomes. A person who leaves the room feeling like the loser—or the winner for that matter—will be a different person when they show up next time.

How do you get a group to move from a place of debate to the place of dialogue?

▶ Tool: Stop the process

How do you travel from a place of debate to a place of dialogue once you deem it appropriate to do so? With questions, of course. As well as a few other tools.

First of all, you need to STOP what is happening as soon as possible (or immediately). Refer back to the section on content and process in Chapter 5 on Empathy and find a way to really STOP things.

> One powerful leader I encountered was leading a group
> sitting in a circle. She got up on her feet and spun around
> slowly with her arms out like a cop who needed to
> manage traffic coming from all directions. Repeatedly
> she said, "Hold on! STOP!" She used her words and her
> body to stop everyone. They were all so worked up that
> they did not see what was happening in the room, and

it even took a few moments for everyone to notice she was standing. If anyone spoke, she would look directly at them, say, "Hold on," with her palm facing them, and maybe a smile. Once everyone was quiet, she ever so slowly backed up to her chair, sat down, took a large inhale of breath, and a big exhale. She used her entire being to stop the process and got the group to look at the process, too. They all knew nothing of value was going to come out of staying in that debate space, and they could see how engrossed they were in it by how much effort it took her to get them back on track.

Now that you have stopped the process, how do you proceed? You can use all the tools available in the **Content** and **Process** section. You can also note what got you to debate and use that to get you back to dialogue. For example, you noticed that people are making some assumptions, and that's how you got to debate; exploring those assumptions can get you back. Let's see what that looks like.

▶ Tool: Question your assumptions

Assumptions can be a real tool for you if you can use them appropriately. Assumptions will inhibit you from being a successful facilitator, especially if the assumptions aren't named. In his book *The Four Agreements*, the textbook I use for my facilitation class, author Don Miguel Ruiz suggests that we should not make assumptions. Even after reading his book, I'm not sure how to do that. What we *can* do is question our assumptions one they are identified. If we can identify what our assumptions are, we can see them as a gift. We can look at that assumption with clarity by opening the gift and turning the assumption into a question. Instead of operating in the background, it takes center stage.

Here are some examples of assumptions turned into questions.

Assumption	Assumption Turned into a Question
They are wrong.	How did we learn these things we feel strongly about?
He did that because he wanted . . .	What compelled him to do that?
We must do X so that Y can happen.	What are other ways we could approach this?
There are two sides to this story.	What perspective, that is not present, could be useful to add to this mix?
Everyone seems to think . . .	So, are we all agreeing that this is true? What else might also be true that we have not discussed?

▶ Tool: Share the other side

I have seen expert facilitators return the group to dialogue and stay in the content by asking individuals to share what the other side is saying (reflective listening?).

> "Bob, I hear you saying that you think . . . Could you also please share what you think Sally is trying to say, without agreeing or disproving what she is trying to say?"

> *Or* "Centrice, I hear that you believe in . . . What does Khay believe in?"

We just covered four tools because they fit so well together that it's hard to take them apart.

- ▸ Notice Debate has happened.
- ▸ Stop the process.
- ▸ Question your assumptions.
- ▸ Share the other side.

Yes, there are lots of traps here. Most of them are connected to awareness.

> **What is the most beautiful sound in the world?**

▶ Trap: Drama caught ya

One possible snafu is not being aware that you are caught up in the drama of the debate. You might be rooting consciously or unconsciously for a particular "side" of the debate. You might find that you are "cheering for" one perspective, hoping for it to "win." If you find yourself saying, "It is about time we are talking about this, now we can get something done," that might be an indicator that you are caught up in the drama.

▶ Antidote: Take all sides

Being a great facilitator or leader often means remaining neutral, or not taking a specific stance, so a wide variety of perspectives can come forward. I suggest, however, that you will be more impactful if you take a stance. In fact, take the stance on all sides. Be quick and nimble, and you'll move toward a variety of perspectives, allowing new insights to flow through the room.

Therefore, if you notice that you are caught up in the drama, investigate which sides of the story are missing.

Make sure that as the facilitator, you are able to move freely from all perspectives and allow all perspectives to come in the room. It is like playing a pickup basketball game in the neighborhood. There is an odd number of people who want to play, and no one wants to sit out. One solution is that one person does not take any allegiance to either side. Her job is to score for whichever team has the ball currently, and she switches quickly whenever the ball changes teams. That would be your job as facilitator—ready to switch sides at a moment's notice to be most useful to ALL players, not just one team. Truth be told, this analogy does not quite work, for it assumes there are only two teams. In reality, the number of teams can be infinite.

▶ Tool: Ask for other perspectives

The antidote, then, is to get other perspectives in the room when you see that the conversation is only revealing a single viewpoint. Ask questions that allow more flavors to be present:

- ▸ Who have we not heard from that could add a different perspective?
- ▸ What are we not saying?
- ▸ Which views are not present?
- ▸ How would this conversation be different if we say more about . . . ? Can we?

Often it can be powerful for the facilitator to state assumptions out loud in a non-judgmental, neutral way. "I am about to ask a question that has an assumption in it. I am assuming we are talking about X and I'm going to ask us to explore how that relates to Y."

▶ Trap: Missing assumptions

Sometimes you may notice that you are caught up in the drama and cannot find an assumption that got you there. You are blind to it. Most likely this is because you made the assumption so quickly you did not see it happen within yourself.

▶ Antidote: Get help seeking the assumption

Sometimes when we get caught up in the drama and have missed the assumption, we feel like we *must* know the way out. Sometimes the best way out is to ask for help and let the group's wisdom lead.

▶ Tool: What is the assumption?

Simply question out loud and let the power of the group come forward. For example:

- ▸ "What assumptions have we made that got us here?"
- ▸ "Who can name some assumptions that they are making right now?"
- ▸ "What are some of us agreeing to as true but have not discussed as true?"

Questions to ask yourself, when a debate is happening in front of you, are:

- ▸ What is it that is really happening here?
- ▸ How might it be useful for the group?

If you can get clear answers to these two questions, you have the ability to make some choices for the group. Often this means going through the process of noticing the debate, stopping the process, asking questions that explore assumptions, and getting folks to share the other side.

Silence

The word LISTEN contains the same letters as the word SILENT.

— Alfred Brendel, classical musician[54] —

Silence is a gift. It is a gift that, once you master giving it, will bring much value to the world and those whom you are serving. Creating silence is a wonderful way to invite people to look deeply in themselves for answers that are beyond regurgitated information. Silence can open the doors to greater understanding. This section examines embracing the power of silence and using it to effectively create a space in which others are invited to share touchy subjects or be more collaborative. It is ironic that I'm writing a book on how to ask powerful questions, because the more I learn and the more I do this work well, the less I actually say.

Silence is needed more often in conversation than we allow for. It can be an invaluable tool when you work up the nerve for it. It does require a certain courage and goes against what is considered "normal." One of the basic tenets of science states that nature abhors a vacuum, and nature is always working to fill a vacuum. People in dialogue also do whatever they can do to fill the vacuum, to fill the silence. When you ask a powerful question, there is an opportunity for silence to exist as people are thinking. Your job is not to break that silence with words. Contribute to it with a smile, with patience, with love, and let the quiet thinking be present.

When you know that you have asked a powerful question, then let it sit. Just let it be. Try not to fix the quiet that follows or make it better; instead, just be.

If you have asked a question and the other person is silent, then it is likely that it is a powerful question and they might be thinking it through—this is safe to assume (we will explore this assumption below: front-loading silence). Be inviting and allow time to pass before expecting a response. Allowing someone, or a group, to be thoughtful is a precious gift. Look at the second hand of your watch, because time will feel like it is standing still for you. You might be thinking, "Oh my gosh, they are not responding. It was such a stupid question. I have to do something."

Often when we ask a question and someone *quickly responds*, we might think, "That was a powerful question." Looking at the answer, though, you will often find that it is full of information, not full of fresh thinking. Sure, you might need to think a little about where you want to go next, but spend most of your time being in the question, too.

▶ Tool: Reading silence

If you have posed what you believe to be a compelling great question and the person or group remains silent or non-responsive, you have a couple of options.

First, notice if their eyes have traveled up or to the side. Do their faces look like they are thinking? If so, be in the silence and let them think.

Secondly, if you cannot read their silence, then let them know that. Simply state, "I don't know how to read your silence." Then let the silence sit some more. They will answer your question eventually. Don't fall into the trap of trying to fix it by immediately rephrasing, filling the space with more words, or suggesting answers they should pick from (like a multiple-choice exam). Let them be in the statement.

Saying "I don't know how to read your silence" is a process-based statement because the facilitator is not talking about the content but referring to their lack of response to the content. I admit that holding this space can be hard, and it is what makes the difference between a good facilitator or leader and a great one. Silent thinking means that something new is happening right now. Let it happen. Let it be created. Let it be shared.

▶ Tool: Front-loading silence

If you expect that the question will make the group think, then you can front-load the silence. Front-loading a question for silence before you ask it invites people to think before they respond. It could sound like this: "I have a question and I would love for us to think about it for minute (yep, a full minute!), in silence, before we respond. At the end of that minute, I will say, *Go*, and then someone can start us off. Here is my question: *In what ways do we not put our customers first?*

It does not need to be a full minute, but it can be. You can suggest any length of time, perhaps fifteen or thirty seconds. Just insert whatever time you think would be most valuable to the group. You could even have them jot ideas down if that would serve them. People can do lots of thinking in fifteen seconds. Moreover, it will serve the timid folks well to think about their own answer before being introduced to others' ideas and responses. Your conversation will have some power of individual thought and be less likely to be full of groupthink.

One way that we as leaders can contribute to group thinking is to ask a powerful question and let someone answer immediately, without any thinking time. As soon as the first person thinks out loud, everyone tends to jump on that bandwagon. If you want more ideas and less consensus, granting time for thinking will allow people to formulate their own ideas.

▶ Trap: Continue to commit to silence

Be sure you are true to your word. Let the silence be a place for thinking. If you promise to dedicate a full minute for this process, then allow a full 60 seconds to expire before moving on. If you say fifteen seconds, honor that amount of time before saying, "Go."

Two things tend to happen when people first use this tool. First, they cut the time shorter than what they said it would be. The silence is too much for them to bear, and they start thinking that more time is not useful. This is especially true for facilitators and leaders whose own style is to think out loud. Don't fall into this trap! Give the group time to think!

The second thing that can happen is that the facilitator lets someone start before they say, "Go." Someone thinks they've got an answer and they are done thinking. They are ready, forgetting for a moment that other people might still be thinking. Your job as a facilitator is to provide feedback (a gesture or a few whispered words) that invites them to honor the quiet space for a while longer. Stopping a person in the group sometimes elicits a chuckle from the groups. That is okay. They will see you as someone who is being true to your word, and that will pay big dividends toward building trust.

Silence is BIG and powerful. Only highly skilled facilitators use it effectively to the group's full advantage. Introverts and extroverts converse differently, especially when new thinking needs to happen. Giving some space for introverts to think allows for more thoughts and ideas. Time will not be wasted; it will be used for thinking. You will have a lot to gain by using this tool.

▶ Tool: Listen first, SPEAK first

If you are really ready to flip things around and you've practiced the above tool and become comfortable with silence, then try this.

> "I have a question and I would love for us to think about it for a minute in silence before we respond. At the end of that minute, I will give some more instructions."

Then state your question slowly and clearly, twice. After your minute of silence, say:

> "Okay, here is the invite: I invite those who tend to speak first to listen first, and those who tend to listen first to speak first."

More silence will follow. That is okay. Everyone will have to adjust to this new paradigm. You may also get some odd responses. If a Talker (and you know they are a Talker) goes first, quickly pause them and say, "You are invited to listen to those who tend to listen first."

This can be tricky to manage. This is one reason to first practice being in the silence. This tool can have a profound impact by creating trust that you want to hear from everyone and that each person's ideas matter.

Notice one thing about this statement: "I invite those who tend to speak first to listen first, and those who tend to listen first to speak first." I could have said, "Those who talk first please wait for those who talk second to go first." The people who tend to talk first are not people who like to wait. Therefore, waiting is not an option for them, really. However, most people understand on some level the value of listening, so asking them to listen gives them something to do.

I have also noticed with some groups it is useful to write the invitation large so everyone can see it. For many, this can be such a new paradigm that it takes them a few moments to wrap their minds around what you are asking, and if they can read the invitation, it is helpful for them to process it.

Most people who talk a lot know they are Talkers. Moreover, they know they tend to go first. Don't be shy about cutting them off. They know that others need to share. They are just wired to go and then go some more. It is your job to remind them of that. They are not going to manage that themselves or may not be able to. They want to contribute, and the way they know how to do that is by talking. So giving them space to listen, which most Talkers are willing to do when reminded to, is a way for them to contribute to the group, too.

▶ Tool: Inviting silence and rapid responses

Another valuable tool is simply inviting silence by presenting a question and then asking that people not answer immediately. There will be some in your group who will appreciate this time to think.

Say something like this:

Step A: "I'm going to ask a question." Take a quick pause to help them see you are about to go slow.

Step B: "After I ask the question, we will take some time to ponder answers in silence before we continue. When I say 'go,' that is the invite answer."

Step C: "You'll each be invited to give a quick answer to the question. We will try to get as many answers from as many of you as possible. Popcorn style. Super quick." Know that when the time comes, some may respond with one word and others with a few sentences.

Step D: "Here's the question: . . ." Then state the question that you would like them to ponder, such as, "What struck you about . . . ?"

Step E: Then do what you said you would do. Wait in silence. Fifteen seconds is not too long; neither is a full minute.

Step F: Say, "Go," and use your body language as an invitation for people to respond.

Step G: Once one person responds, say, "Thank you," and go quickly to the next person.

Let people share openly for the popcorn round but don't dig deep. Reflect back to the individual or group when needed but make it clear that you are trying to get lots of ideas in the room quickly.

You may need to reflect many times while the popcorn is popping. You are trying to affirm those who threw something into the room and reflect them back while also listening for two things:

1. any theme or idea that connects many of the thoughts
2. any reaction that incites multiple reactions (group exhale, chuckles, words of support), indicating that it is a hot topic worthy of exploring more deeply

One word of caution: Do not immediately go the topic that created the most reaction. Allow for more responses so as many people as possible can participate right off the bat, and test if the reaction was just a fluke or actually the way this group responds.

When you use the tool and go through these steps, it is important that you have a clear transition between the popcorn round and the start of the dialogue, so that people understand you have moved away from the quick pace. Do it clearly with your words and your body language. You might even move your hands more slowly. When you pause the group, reflect back on themes you heard come up repeatedly, or think about how their comments might be connected. (You can also ask them if they noticed any themes themselves.) Then ask a question, which at the core has the theme you heard during the earlier popcorn session. Notice how they respond as you go forward.

Those steps would continue like this:

Step H: Avoid the temptation to dive deeply into any one person's response.

Step I: When everyone has responded (ideally) or you get enough responses to see a theme with connections between what people have said, stop the popcorn and reflect that theme.

Step J: Ask a powerful question on that theme, and make your intention clear that we are now diving deep into deeper answers (no longer popcorn).

Managing silence by utilizing the above tools invites a fresh dialogue to happen. In this way, silence is a powerful tool of contemplation. It is rare. Oftentimes if we've got fifteen seconds of silence, we engage with someone or—more commonly now—with a small electronic device that affirms our presence (and maybe love) in the world. The brain works amazingly quickly, so allowing for a fifteen-second break can be rewarding. Rather than focusing on new information coming in, you invite the brain to focus on what is present. Once given permission and a chance to "reset," the brain will create original thoughts instead of recirculating and regurgitating the thoughts others have expressed verbally.

On the other hand, the first person who speaks may begin the process of thinking out loud because they are comfortable and have a lot of practice verbalizing their thoughts. However, a consequence of letting them think out loud is that their ramblings will have a direct impact on the brains of others in the room. Rather than giving other folks time to think, their brains are now connecting to these new thoughts and making choices about what to share (oftentimes based on your or others' reactions). How people react in the room often has a powerful and immediate influence on people's unformulated and incomplete thoughts. It also allows them to get attached enough to these thoughts that they may be less inclined to dismiss them as they see how people react to someone immediately thinking out loud.

This is a simple tool to counteract groupthink. If you notice that people are all saying the same thing, you might be contributing to this dynamic. Without even noticing, you might be giving too much power to the first people who speak.

If you notice groupthink happening, you can simply ask, "What thoughts are contrary to what we have heard so far?" This will allow someone to go back to where they were and share those thoughts.

If you have asked a powerful question that automatically leads to silence with no prompt from you, that is okay. You might start squirming, but remember they're just thinking. Let them think.

Rather than squirm, I have seen talented facilitators do the following things:

- Wait in the silence, too. Just be in it with them.
- Smile and make lots of eye contact with the group members.
- Say something like, "I appreciate the silence and assume it means you're seriously thinking about the question. Let's take some more silence to wrestle with these thoughts in our minds before we wrestle with them as a group."
- Say, "Thanks for thinking."

▶ Tool: Unreadable silence
There is one tool I pull out in rare moments when the silence is really heavy. "Heavy" silence is when people start to exhibit

avoiding body language (i.e., looking away, looking at other things outside the circle, excessive shifting of weight). If this is the case, I've found that making the following statement helps—of course, followed by silence:

"I don't know how to read your silence," or "I don't know how to respond to your silence."

▶ Trap: Fixing silence

The trap involves fixing it or trying to make it better. If you know your question is a worthwhile question to explore, and you know it's something that the group needs to talk about, then stay present. Try not to hide or let the group hide. Hiding occurs commonly in these three ways:

1. The facilitator tries to fix the silence with more words—more words that are often not needed.
2. The facilitator allows the group members to change the topic rather than truly answer the question.
3. Someone in the group throws a question back at the facilitator: "What do you mean by that question?" It sounds as if they are making an assumption that you are making an implication.

▶ Antidote: Be silent and restate intention

Resist the urge to fill the silence. This is a skill that takes time and practice. If you feel you *must* fill the silence, try, "I don't know how to respond to your silence," and then just wait.

You might also establish what your intent is. For instance,

"My intent in asking this question is to explore the impact that X has on us as a group." Then wait in silence. Look at a second hand or count slowly (one one thousand, two one thousand, . . .), get to at least fifteen, but thirty or even sixty seconds are even better. Do anything you can to keep from breaking the silence again, even if that means you have to sit on your hands to keep from breaking the silence.

By stating your intention, you will help alleviate reluctance stemming from a lack of clarity. They might not want to answer due to who is in the room—a boss, for example—and stating your intent can help address the bigger "why" and its importance, allowing their purpose to rule over any fear that is arising.

What else could I say that would help you understand the value of silence? If silence scares you, then think of it as "thinking time." A result of asking a powerful question is the magic that happens once that question has been asked. If it is a truly powerful question, then people will be thinking, and they will be thinking about new things or old things in new ways. Let them think. It is powerful. If you have done a good job of establishing rapport, then most people will appreciate some time with you to think. This will be doubly so if you want to hear how people respond to your question. They will sense desire. People love to be heard. Give them space to share some new thoughts.

Sitting in silence is a way of honoring the presence of the others, even if they are really busy. Slowing down to think fresh and new is a real treat that most people will appreciate. However, in this fast-paced world, some will need a reminder of the value of slowing down. Most often, being clear about your intent will be a great reminder for them, and for some, you might need to be really blunt: "Let's slow down and think this though. What could this mean for you?"

MORE about silence: Silence may feel awkward. I even hear people calling silence out by using words like "awkward" or, now, "awkward turtle." How the turtle ever got involved with awkward I don't know, but it is a shame. In his book *The Broken Truth*, children's author Douglas Wood makes the turtle a character of wisdom. Silence can be the place of wisdom if we own it and let people step into it.

▸ Tools: Stepping into silence
Ways that I step into the silence:

> I say, "We are going to take a moment to consider our thoughts on this matter before speaking so we are in touch with our own thoughts before we are influenced by the thoughts of others."

> When silence happens without me suggesting it in a more formal way, I will own it if it's useful for the group. I might say, "I'm guessing, based on the silence, that people are thinking. Great. Let's take some more time to think in silence, and when someone is ready to share, feel free to do so." Or, I might say, "Based on the silence, I'm guessing that people are thinking. Great. Let's take another thirty seconds and continue to really settle into the silence and your thinking. When I say, *Go*, anyone can share when they are ready."

I might also just smile, nod, and wait in silence. People tend not to let silence go for too long before speaking.

Along the way, our public school system has led us to believe that silence equates to being stupid or ignorant. Students who could answer the teacher's question most quickly were rewarded, while those of us who could not answer immediately endured the wrath of "stupid" jokes from peers and teachers alike. Let's create space where people are encouraged to think individually and then collectively.

Silence is the house in which wisdom lives. Invite yourself over, sit down, have a cup of tea, and learn something new.

Web Building

We don't accomplish anything in this world alone . . .
and whatever happens is the result of the whole tapestry
of one's life and all the weavings of individual threads
from one to another that creates something.

— Sandra Day O'Connor[55] —

This next strategy for asking powerful questions allows for direct connection among members of the group. We will call this web building, for it is as if a spiderweb is connecting the different people in the room. We could define web building as doing anything that gets people to talk to each other directly, that gets them connected to each other. As a leader or a facilitator, you can make lots of magic happen, if people are talking directly with each other and being real. Participants talking directly to each other is much more powerful than people getting up on their soapboxes and preaching what they think or know. When each person is actually responding—as well as connecting—to the person and what has been said, something real happens and new ideas and thoughts can be created.

The spiderweb analogy can go further. Have you ever noticed, while walking across a grassy field early in the morning, that there are little spiderwebs that were not there yesterday? I would guess those spiderwebs were there yesterday but one could not see them. The morning dew brings the spiderweb into view. In the same way, when a group of people walk into a room, there are invisible connections between them. These connections won't be visible to the different people until the "dew" can capture the light and make the connections visible. What can you do to make those connections visible to all in the room? Create the dew.

▶ Trap: Focus is all on the leader or facilitator

Early in the process of managing groups, sometimes the leader will unconsciously turn the room's attention to themselves. They are not aware that in doing so, they are stealing a valuable asset. That asset is the connection that exists between other people in the room. It is so easy to do this that we are unaware that it is even happening.

It's easy to steal connections and hold the group's focus directly by saying things like:

- "Okay folks, I'm here to ask you some questions. Please respond to my questions with honest answers."
- "My job here is to find a solution to this important problem. Let's talk about it and maybe I can hear a solution that I can take up the ladder."

Can you hear where the focus is? In these examples, the focus is on the leader, even if that is not their intent. When the focus is on the leader, there is a great chance that a dialogue will become a Q&A session.

▶ Antidote: Let the focus be on the people

The job of the leader is to focus the group's attention on the individuals that comprise the group and, if attention becomes directed toward the leader, to shift the focus back to the group. This requires first developing clarity around the intention, sharing the intention, and then steering the ship with firm hands. The following tools show examples of ways to Ask, Tell, Show, Reflect, and Hold as a way to get people to talk with each other rather than with you as the leader. The result is that they may be more honest and open, sharing with a member of the group or with the leader listening in, as compared to sharing directly with the leader and being put "on the spot."

▶ Tool: Creating the dew—making connections visible

Here are some things I do and have seen others do to make connections visible in the room, with a fair amount of success:

Ask: The first option may be obvious, but it's rarely done and relatively easy. Say something like, "Can you respond directly to Jackie?" or "Would you please respond to what you hear Jackie saying?" You are asking them to speak directly to each other. Sometimes in a group setting, especially when the topic is intense, this is difficult for people to do unless they are asked. They need an invitation in order to address the fear of directly talking to each other. Once invited, this suddenly seems completely natural.

Tell: Sometimes it's valuable to be more directive: "Please talk directly to Jackie; she is right here to listen." I tend to do this most often when members of the group are looking at me each time they talk, rather than looking at others in the room. By giving a clear directive to one, or to the whole group, it sends a clear message of "Remember we can talk to each other because we are all present in the room."

Show: Sometimes the best thing is to do *something* but say nothing. "Doing the dew" is what I call it. The "something" I do uses lots of body language and lets the group explore the connections.

> *I was facilitating a group around the topic of race in which a black female stated that she could not see any "light at the end of tunnel." She felt the world was stacked against her. She could not see how she was going to pay her bills and do all that was expected of her. A few moments later, a white male described his strategy for how he makes the light come closer, adding it was not a big deal to feel lost for a moment. "When that happens, I just need to focus."*
>
> *In response to these two comments being in the room, I wanted these two to speak directly to each other. I was making connections in my mind and I was confident that the black female thought, "just focus would be easy if you were white." Rather than suggest a connection myself, I just looked at the two of them, said, "Black female," looking toward her, then looked at him and said, "White male," then held out each of my hands in an inviting way to each of them (palms facing out, fingertips pointed at them). I took my hands, turned them into pointing fingers, and pointed them at the other. I was basically saying, "you two talk directly to each other," but I did it without verbally speaking.*

It worked. She went on to say that, in her world, "no light at the end of the tunnel is more the norm." He went on to say how in his world it is not. Every day, she is focused and working really hard just to get by: "How am I going to pay my bills?" For him, life offered itself on a silver platter if he only asked for it. Meaningful dialogue happened because they were able to make the connection to each other.

As this example demonstrates, the connections are not always similarities between people, but can be differences, too. If two people stand on different ends of a spectrum of thought, there is a connection between them in the same way that a spiderweb connects two different blades of grass. I "did the dew" by encouraging them to string that web, not forcing the connection by telling them what I saw.

Reflect: When wanting to connect different people in the room and get them to talk directly to each other, it is a good time to use reflective listening. In this instance, the reflective listening method will most commonly be Connecting the Dots, but in this case, you are not connecting different points within one person. You are connecting different ideas, thoughts, and/or stories and helping the individuals in the room relate to them as a theme. You then hold that theme for the group and you find ways to connect that theme to individuals in the room.

> For example, you have been hearing different experiences in the room but are not sure that people see how they related. You help the group by saying, "I am hearing Jackie say . . . and Jose say . . . and Julie say . . . What is the connection between these experiences, and in what ways might that be true for others in the room?"

Remember that making connections is not just getting people to respond to others' ideas but getting them to engage with the persons in the room by talking *directly* to them. Deep connection is people responding directly and naturally by listening. In a true dialogue, you don't want people to prescribe or give advice on how to "fix" whatever has come forward.

Hold: Related to reflecting is something that I call *holding*. When you hear someone say something that is powerful or profound or just hits you in some kind of way, your job is to grab it and hold it up for the world to see or feel. This would be easy if words were objects and you could actually hold them up, but instead, you have to do everything you can to make it seem as if you could actually pick up the words.

> *I was facilitating a group one time when a black woman said that she felt like she could not talk the way she was taught to talk as a child—language punctuated with the heavy urban slang and abbreviated diction common in inner-city ghettos. I asked her if she would take a risk and talk with us in that way, so we would have an understanding of what it would sound like. She agreed, with reluctance. When she spoke, she picked up the collar of her shirt as if trying to hide. In response, some in the group chuckled and others were beginning to take the humor and go somewhere else with it, chatting amongst themselves. Meanwhile under her breath, she said she felt like an idiot talking that way, but her words got lost in the chuckles in the room.*

I responded by saying in a big, serious voice, "Did you all hear that?" (with a big pause) "That was huge!" I paused again and made eye contact with everyone, then fixed my eyes on her: "Would you mind saying again what you just said? For I believe it's truly important for all of us to really hear you."

The room became dead quiet and everyone looked at her. She looked at me and I gave a little head nod of encouragement. I was letting her know, "I got your back, sister," as best as I could with my eyes. Fully aware that I was asking her to admit to "feeling like an idiot" one more time, and trusting that holding that word for everyone would serve the group.

Quietly, holding up the collar of her shirt to cover her mouth she said, "I feel like an idiot talking like that. Like you won't understand me." Then she twisted in her seat, so she was no longer facing the group.

I took it from there. I let the silence sit for moment and said, "Did you hear that?" I paused and took a long loud exhale. "She feels like an idiot if she talks the way she was taught. She feels like an idiot if she talks 'black.' Imagine what that would be like, not able to be fully yourself. Feel that!"

I was silent for some time and it was in that silence that a white man looked at me and then at her, then back at me. I gave him a brief head nod, encouraging him to explore his curiosity.

"What does it require of you to speak 'white'?" he said softly. Then after taking a quick glance my way, as if to ask, "Was that okay?" he turned back to her and said a little louder, *"What parts of yourself have been sacrificed to 'fit in' with society?"*

She looked at him with penetrating eyes and he held her gaze. He whispered, "I really want to know."

She twisted back toward the group, let out a loud exhale, looked at the group as if checking to see if this was real and said, "No one has ever asked me that before." She dropped her collar, her hands moving as rapidly as the words coming out of her mouth, openly sharing the thoughts that had been kicking around in her head but never expressed out loud. "I'm not really sure because I never was able to think clearly about it but . . ." Engagement then was real and present.

Holding can be a powerful way to help members of the group engage. It is your job to remind the group why they are gathered and then invite them to step fully into that commitment. I often hold by asking someone to repeat their sentiments, by reflecting powerful words, asking for silence, stating the intended objectives, or by returning to important subject matter that might have gotten lost as the conversation moved forward.

Use Names: One of the simplest ways to get people to talk directly to each other is to use their names and ask others in the room to use names, too. Depending on what kind of gathering it is, ask yourself if it's okay for them to wear nametags. In groups that you work with often, you might ask them to wear nametags well past the point at which everyone should know each other's names. This technique gives them no excuse for not using names. Often when things are tough and dicey, when emotions are high, the person who is speaking will do a quick glance at a nametag before they say someone's name. They know the name, but it's easy to forget when things are tense, when emotions rule. With nametags, participants don't need to worry about making a mistake, and the focus can be on the connection or content.

You can use participants' names in several ways.

When reflective listening to a person directly:

"Beth, you are saying . . ."

When taking someone's comments and giving them to the group:

"So Beth said . . . And that leads me to ask you all . . ."

When someone reflects on comments from the group but uses pronouns or vague words like "someone said," you can ask, "Who said that?" The subtle and small interjections will often help the group use each other's names more often, even if you don't directly say, "Use each other's names."

Use the participant's names as much as possible and ask them to do so as well—then the connections will happen.

As the leader, if someone's name is odd to you, don't be shy—ask for the correct pronunciation. Chances are, you won't be the only one struggling to get it right. The fact that you are interested in knowing the correct pronunciation shows people that you care enough to get it right and really want get to know someone. This will be helpful to others and give them the encouragement to try different names, too.

Other Useful Ways to Web Build

All of the skills we have been practicing as we have travelled up the Pyramid have a way of coming together at the top. If you are having a difficult time getting people to connect and have real dialogue with each other, all you need to do is travel down the Pyramid. Sometimes if things have been going well, you might only need to go one level down. Other times you might find that you need to "reset" or "restart" by going to the base and working back up. Some questions you might ask yourself are:

- ▸ How could I, as a facilitator, have contributed to this group dynamic?
- ▸ Have I been clear about your intention?
- ▸ Have I established rapport and helped others to connect?
- ▸ Am I open and asking questions that are open-ended and inviting people to explore together?
- ▸ Am I listening and reflecting cleanly or with judgment?
- ▸ Am I being empathic? Am I encouraging others to be empathic?

Defining Words

How, when and what you perceive—defines your life!

— Ramana Pemmaraju[56] —

When in conversation, it is common for someone to want a word to be defined. If you're facilitating, asking people to define words is not as useful as it might seem. Any person in the group can ask for a word to be defined, but when the facilitator does it, it creates a power dynamic that becomes sticky—the facilitator has become "the expert" looking for a correct answer. On the other hand, when a member of the group asks for something to be defined, it creates an opportunity to work together deeply. Here is one way that I play with it.

In a group, a black man used the word "whitewash" to describe how he defaults to speaking like his classmates, rather than speaking like he would in the city that he is from. Another classmate asked him what whitewashing meant. Rather than let him define it, I said, "Rather than Trent defining the word 'whitewashing' right now, I would like to first ask something of all of you'. Something came to your mind when he used the word. What was that? Also, earlier Diamond used the term 'acting white' to describe her experience of being here as a black woman. Let's share what we understand by those words and then we will go back and ask them to define what they meant by them."

As a result, something funny happened. Many of the white people spoke, saying what they thought about it or what that experience must be like. No other people of color spoke till nearly all the white people spoke. Than the people of color (other than black) spoke with an intensity rarely seen before. Their experience with whitewash was quite different. Finally, I asked Trent and Diamond to speak about what they meant by whitewash, and their definitions were yet again quite different from anyone else's. We had so much diversity of definition in the room by that point, that a fruitful conversation ensued.

What I might have done was allow the black man to define the word as he used it, supporting the other participant's question. However, asking the group to speak about their perception of whitewashing encouraged their curiosity and allowed them to wrestle with the topic of race in the room (and not some theory just in their heads). Race was then not something "out there" and separate, but alive and present. By bringing in Diamond's language, "acting white," and combining it with the term "whitewashing," I helped ensure that our group dynamic was not about individual thoughts. It was about an experience that multiple people in the room were enduring in their daily lives.

Managing the Overtalkers

Relentless rain, like a non-stop talker.

— Marty Rubin[57] —

We all have been to meetings in which there is someone who has lots to say, and others are not saying much. No one knows what to do. It's not that this person is trying to be dominating; they are just talking or thinking out loud, or they don't have their thoughts together.

The dominant talkers *know* that they talk a lot. They know that they often go first and most of them know that there is value in letting others share. They are simply well practiced at talking. So help them and help others in the room. Remedy the situation by following these steps.

Step 1: <u>Stop</u> them. You will need to interrupt them. This can be the hardest part. Less experienced facilitators might wait until there is a lull or a thought is completed. That could take a *long* time if the person is on a tangent or thinking out loud. If you have been able to remain in a neutral position and found yourself thinking, "I wish this person would stop talking," you are not the only one in the room thinking that. When it's valuable to the group for a person to stop talking, then you must find a way to stop them sooner rather than later.

When I'm leading, I will often use the word "pause." A colleague of mine uses the word "stop." You can also use some kind of body language, like in the earlier story where a colleague acted as a traffic cop in order to redirect emotions.

"Can I pause you right there?" or "Let me pause you."

"Hold on. Stop right there." *(Be attentive to your tone—it will have a huge impact.)*

Step 2: <u>Affirm</u> them if you can do it genuinely. Faking is not allowed.

"Thank you for sharing."
"Thank you for being so forthright with your thoughts."
"Jake, I love how you can think so quickly about new material."

Step 3: <u>Reflect</u> what you heard, using the tools of reflective listening. If you want to be sure they don't keep going, use a short Verbatim reflection.

"I heard you say . . ."

Step 4 (optional): Invite the group to <u>respond</u> to what the speaker said.

"Let's see how others respond to what you are saying."
"What do others think about what Jake is saying?"

Sometimes with very chatty folks, you need to introduce Step 4 before you actually do Step 3. That might sound like this with all the steps:

JAKE "I think that American history clearly says why we are here. You must know what has happened in the past to be able to predict the present. In addition, what it says is . . . We should have known this was going to happen. There has always been some group of people that we oppressed: the Native Americans, the Blacks, the Mexicans, the Jews. And yet . . ."

YOU "Hold on, Jake. Thank you for sharing. I want to also see what others are thinking about what you said and the original question. You are saying that American history could easily predict this present moment. Okay, folks: what are your thoughts?"

In addition, if acronyms are helpful for you to be able to do this, use SARR: Stop, Affirm, Redirect, Respond. When fear arises over stopping someone, it has been helpful for me to remember two things:

1. The talker is okay with it.
2. The rest of the group will be grateful for your actions.

If you feel like they have talked too long, the rest of the group feels it, too. The health of the whole group is at risk if you let them continue. It is all right to interrupt them from a loving space.

Steering into the Curve

Slowly it dawned on me that steering into the curve,
in this instance, is about seeing opportunities hidden in
what at first may appear to be problems!

— Christopher Uhl[58] —

There comes a point at which the skills you have been learning start to sink in and more powerful questions show up in your life. If you really want to take your ability to the next level, there is a skill that needs to be added. Some of my colleagues call this "Steering into the Curve," and it works best after you have been practicing what you have learned so far and have confidence in these skills. As you began to do this work, you might have noticed your curiosity became heightened. This curiosity might make you aware of things that you are scared to touch or confront. This new skill requires you to face your demons and the demons of many in the room. It requires you to lean into the fear rather than run away from it. It requires you to be fully present to what is, rather than dreaming about what could be. It requires you to look for, grab, and hold the very thing that is so scary that most people will not even acknowledge that it exists. Finally, it requires that you hold that fear (whatever it is) in such a way that others can talk about it, bringing meaning to everyone.

It is a huge challenge. If you have been working your way up the Pyramid, you are ready. You might have already done it and not be aware that you have done so.

What is it? It is grasping hold of the very thing that is underneath the content of the conversation, that is influencing the conversation, and bringing it forth so that we all can talk about it in a heathy way. These questions will help you:

- ▸ What is the unspoken thing that is driving us in this conversation (or in life)?
- ▸ What factors are influencing us that make this topic challenging?

My father, who was a racecar driver, taught me how to Steer into the Curve. When your car begins to skid and lose traction, firmly grasp the wheel and turn the wheel in the direction of the skid, even if it means you are now pointing your wheel directly into the mountain wall, and do this until you get traction back. Even then, continue to correct. Although this practice is counterintuitive, it has prevented me from spinning out of control while driving on icy roads in the dead of winter. Once while driving on a tight off-ramp leaving the highway, I found my back end going to the left. Now, under my tires I had an invisible ice patch. Had I continued to keep my front tires turned right to go around the curve, I would have spun around 360 degrees until I hit something or my momentum was used up. Instead, Dad's teaching showed up and I turned my wheel to the left, pointing right at the guardrail, "steering into the curve." My back end was no longer skidding to the left, and I turned my wheel to the right slowly to finish going around the curve.

Often, we steer conversations along the road we assume is smooth. We are going along peacefully when something happens that impacts the conversation, like black ice on the highway. Our tendency is to pretend nothing happened, to push through with the agenda, to get the work done. However, more often than not, the black ice is where the real work is. If we pretend the black ice does not exist, the conversation or project will spin out of control until the momentum is all used up. More useful is to steer into the curve and authentically name what you see, or ask a question about the thing that is influencing the conversation. This may mean leaving the content for a moment and asking a process-based question.

> Once I was working with a CEO who'd been in place for about two months following several other managers who had been in the same position, all for brief periods of time. In his mind, he thought working seven a.m. to eleven p.m. would prove to his team that he was the one CEO who would be sticking around. As he continued to tell me about projects he was working on that were not going so well, I paused him and asked, "Do your employees know that you have a wife and two kids?" He was shocked that I'd inserted this personal question into a conversation about innovation and workflow.
>
> Reluctantly, with a quizzical look on his face, he said, "Yes."
> I continued: "And do they know that your family lives two thousand-plus miles away?"
> "Yes."
> "And that they have not moved here?"

"Yes."

"What might that mean to your team? What conclusions might they jump to regarding how committed you are to remaining with this organization and projects you're initiating here?"

"They all know I'm committed," he said, raising his voice.

"Ah, hold on here for a second. I'm asking you to answer a question that might shift how you see your new company and employees. What might it mean to your team that your family is still not here?"

With a breath, he realized that his employees might not view his long days as a commitment to the team, but rather as an attempt to get the results as quickly as possible so he could quickly move on to the next position in a new city, like his predecessors had done. Steering into the curve helped him see one reason he was not getting any traction with the new projects he was trying to implement.

If the Steering into the Curve analogy does not work for you, try Leaning into the Fear, or Holding the Taboo, or Naming the Elephant. The point is to address the underlying assumptions that are driving the dialogue and that people are not brave enough to address alone. Your role in Steering into the Curve is to help others be brave enough to confront the unspoken fear. In the space between the "fear of addressing it" and "courage to do something about it" is you and one breath. Authentically take a dive in, be clear about your intention at every point that it seems useful, and ask.

Working with Co-Facilitators

We live by each other and for each other.
Alone we can do so little. Together we can do so much.

— Helen Keller[59] —

Frequently, when we think of "leading," we think of one person leading. I suggest that two people who are adept at the skills presented in this book can do much more service to a group than one person alone. Two people can create something that neither could do by themselves.

- ▸ Some results of collaborating with another facilitator: When one facilitator's triggers get hit, the other facilitator might be able to move ahead with ease to bypass the emotional response of his or her co-facilitator.
- ▸ Every facilitator has a listening style that focuses on particular things. By having two facilitators, one of them will catch something the other has missed.
- ▸ Questions become clearer to the group. If one facilitator asks a question and the second facilitator can see it caused some confusion, they can state the question in a different way that will dispel that confusion.

This can be done best if co-facilitators connect before working with each other. Often this means taking time before each dialogue to talk about what is important for them in that moment. It might be what they are working on to become better. What is discussed is less important than actually connecting. It is also useful for them to share after each dialogue what they were think-ing during critical moments so that they can become better at un-derstanding how they may have contributed to group dynamics.

One thing that can scare new facilitators who are working together is talking to each other live in front of the group. What that might look like is one facilitator saying directly to the other, "Let me pause this conversation for a moment, folks. Sam [your co-facilitator], I'm curious about where we are going right now. It looks like we are headed down this path . . . (say a bit of what you see). I wonder if it would be more useful for the group to head down this other path . . . (say a bit about what you envi-sion). What are you thinking?" This live dialogue is useful for everyone in the room. It does not need to be whispered while the group is doing something else. Ideally, your co-facilitator is sitting on the other side of the circle so you can each see things the other cannot. (Yes, it is best to get your knights to show up to the round table, but, lacking a carpenter to build the table, just getting people to sit in a circle without a table is far better than sitting in lecture format. The point is the *roundness*, not the table, so that each person knows by the room setup that they have an equal voice. Often, I prefer no table at all.)

Summary

A human being is a part of the whole, called by us "Universe,"
a part limited in time and space. He experiences himself,
his thoughts and feelings as something separated from
the rest, a kind of optical delusion of his consciousness.
This delusion is a kind of prison for us, restricting us to our
personal desires and to affection for a few persons nearest
to us. Our task must be to free ourselves from this prison
by widening our circle of compassion to embrace all living
creatures and the whole of nature in its beauty.

— Albert Einstein[60] —

Here is the point in the book where it all comes together. The reality, however, is that this is a journey in which the destination is always out there in front of you. Asking powerful questions is a skill that you get to work on for the rest of your life. Asking yourself and others questions that make a difference will transform how you see the world.

Each layer of the Pyramid has two ways to describe what is happening in that layer. These sentences in themselves summarize the book well.

EMPATHY	I feel with you
LISTENING	I get you
OPENNESS	I hear you
RAPPORT	I see you
INTENTION	I am willing to know you

Starting at the base of the Pyramid: People want to know that there are others willing to know them. They want to be seen. They want to be heard. They want for people to "get" them and be really understood. They want to know that others feel what they feel. By asking powerful questions to those around you, you can start exploring worlds other than just your own. Your world will open up and you will see things you did not see before. People will feel connected. Moreover, from that place we can begin to make a difference.

So you might be asking, "Why does the top of the Pyramid have a '*We!*'?" Maybe you caught yourself and rephrased it to, "*What* is the meaning of the "We!" at the top?" What do *you* think it might mean?

You might have noticed that as you traveled down this journey, a mind shift has occurred. Have you noticed it? How has your thinking shifted? There have been tools along the way that supported you on your journey. Consider these, for example:

- creating intentions that stretch you to include the needs of others
- following your natural, genuine curiosity when connecting
- shifting from judgment to openness by dropping why-based questions
- listening for anything, rather than listening to how you might be right
- describing how they see the world

Each of these tools invites us to shift our mindset from "me" to "We!"

A *We!*™ mindset considers and values the needs of the others, allowing them to fully express their own humanity. This journey has been an invite to step into a place of mastery. Not a mastery over others, but a mastery of being with others in such a way that everyone is enriched and supported by the experience.

Imagine a board meeting in which a transformative idea comes forth. Once brought to light, everyone in the room takes turns offering input and contributes something that adds to the idea, giving it more and more traction as brainstorming takes over the room. In the end, the only true author then becomes, "We!" No one person can honestly claim that they were the author, for the idea was brought to life by every individual in the room. You are now invited to become a master of the *We!*™ mindset. To be present to the possibility of what *We!*™ can create together. Become a Weologist and be connected to all that surrounds you.

This *We!*™ mindset takes practice to develop. And yet, we all have the ability to be in a *We!*™ mindset simply by choosing to be so. We all have reasons to jump into our me mindset, fear being be the driver who takes us there, often without us being aware. Now you can choose to become the master. Simply name the fear, ask it to sit in the passenger seat, and drive like it matters. Like a mastery archer who becomes the target, the bow, the arrow, and breathe, all in one moment. The *We!*™ mindset allows you to connect with, "to become," all the characters in the drama of your own life.

So often we spend our lives trying to separate ourselves from those around us. Choose to be a Weologist. Practice these tools present here.

You will find as you master them that there will be exceptions to each of the rules, otherwise known as traps. For example, there will be times when a closed question will be perfect (like when emotions are intense). Your ability to discern whether the timing is perfect will come with practice. The top of the Pyramid is where you masterfully apply the skills and make them your own.

Successful students all have one thing in common—they showed up with a spirit of playfulness. I'm not meaning they showed up in clown shoes, though sometimes that might help. I mean that they moved into a world in which *right* and *wrong* are less important than curiosity, where looking good is less important than helping someone else look good, where rules are less important than being present to what shows up now in the moment. You have the skills now to create the conversations that matter by asking powerful questions that arise in the present moment. There is no one size fits all.

Asking a complete stranger a question that dives deep into a place of curiosity is similar to a child on the playground asking a potential new friend if he wants to play a game of "Let's Pretend." Asking those questions is outside the norms of the day-to-day where we pretend to be dead to what is alive around us. When we ask powerful questions, we awaken deep connections in which *right* and *wrong* are no longer the house rules. It is a game changer. The boredom, the humdrum of life, is awakened to something new and fresh. Children are adept at taking what is available to them in the present and making it part of a fun game. We can learn to do the same in our own lives. To learn from the children of the world. To remember what it was like to play, where you were not focused on making mistakes. Go out and play with the concepts and skills presented here, and watch new possibilities appear. Bring forth a spirit of playfulness. Play with questions.

The best way to kill a question is with an answer. Arm yourself with powerful questions that have no immediate answer and just sit with them for a while. Chew on them. Ask them of others before you begin your next meal. Delight in the unknown. Be an explorer of the unknown that surrounds us. Create conversations that matter.

Share your stories at www.askpowerfulquestions.com.

What is the most adventurous thing you have ever done?

What has been your greatest accomplishment so far?

Acknowledgments

Writing a book is an act of practiced perseverance. So many times, I have wanted to quit writing this book. The only two things that kept me going were the community holding me up by saying things like "I want to read it" or "Yes, that is worth sharing" and a deep desire to have people *connect*, really connect.

It is so hard to sit with focused time and clearly get what I want across, without seeing the face of the reader, to know if it has landed correctly. I could use the rest of this page to let you know how this is such an impossible task or . . . to thank all the people who made it possible. That sounds like more fun.

First of all, my family. My second set of parents, Ken and Linda Wise, who gave me a chance to be something, whose major gift was to get out of the way and allow us boys to be whatever we wanted to be. With my learning disabilities, none of us ever thought I would write a book. My Uncle Don and Aunt Lynne, who taught me to hold onto an idea I believed in, no matter how contrary to societal views. My wife, Heather, who has been an impossibly huge support though this process whilst writing her own book, managing her own business, and having a "long-term pro bono leadership contract" with three of the greatest kids on the planet. She has carved time so I was able to write. Thanks for giving up so much so I could get these words out there. Gratitude to my three very young kids, Cypress, Fern, and Sylvan, who made it possible (and easy) to be a dad first and make work second.

On the professional front, Dr. Sam Richards and Dr. Laurie Mulvey have been the most supportive bosses I have ever known. Their ability to allow all kinds of people to reach their full potential is amazing and is an inspiration for all of us. There is a long line of teachers who have co-taught this material with me over the years, each of whom has given invaluable contributions: Sheffy Minnick, Trent Hall, Chiluvya Zulu, Lulu Ahumada, Brandon Munroe, Michele Frisby, Eden Araya, Brenton Mitchell, Danna Jayne (DJ) Seballos, Salim George, Carly Cubit, Merin Briggs, and Jenny Beben. There is also a long list of "students" who have been amazing teachers to me and to their classmates. Thank you for your willingness to show up so fully and engage.

To Chad Littlefield, my partner in contributing to making a difference in the world. Your ability to connect and make others look good is amazing. You are truly a gift to the world. And thanks to Alyzah Lozano for helping to keep all the details of *We and Me Inc.* together.

When people call me an author, it would be more accurate to say, "Employer of editors." I wrote some stuff that was unreadable. Somehow, editors found a way to make it digestible. Paula Hofmeister, who has an amazing amount of patience and love. Kirstin Waldkoenig was able to show up fully, filling in the holes—thank you for your full engagement in this project. Rebecca Thomas had tons of patience as she coached me through the places where the text was still sticky, and Sunny DiMartino is a whiz with all things creative; her superpower is taking the ideas of others making them beautiful (graphics). Thank you. Also, to a number of other editors and early readers who had a great influence on places the text needed help: Beth Gross, Heather House, Carly Cubit, and Chris Uhl.

To the major teachers in my life, Allen Cohen, the Mastery Foundation, Jamie and Maren Showkier, Tom Brown Jr., S.N. Goenka and all his teachers, the Peace Corps and the amazing people of Nepal, and Rod Lee, a great teacher in how to be a leader.

Notes

Endnotes

1   Sam Keen, *In the Absence of God: Dwelling in the Presence of the Sacred* (New York: Harmony, 2010), 56.

2   Knvul Sheikh, "Most Adults Spend More Time on Their Digital Devices Than They Think," *Scientific American*, March 1, 2017, https://www.scientificamerican.com/article/most-adults-spend-more-time-on-their-digital-devices-than-they-think/.

3   Sherry Turkle, "The Flight From Conversation," *New York Times*, April 21, 2012, https://www.nytimes.com/2012/04/22/opinion/sunday/the-flight-from-conversation.html.

4   David Whyte, "Life at the Frontier: The Conversational Nature of Reality," February 26, 2011, TED video, 19:13, https://www.youtube.com/watch?v=5Ss1HuA1hlk.

5   Geoff MacDonald and Lauri A. Jensen-Campbell, eds., *Social Pain: Neuropsychological and Health Implications of Loss and Exclusion* (Washington, D.C.: American Psychological Association, 2010).

6   Karyn Twaronite, "The Surprising Power of Simply Asking Coworkers How They're Doing," *Harvard Business Review*, February 28, 2019, https://hbr.org/2019/02/the-surprising-power-of-simply-asking-coworkers-how-theyre-doing.

7   Karyn Twaronite, "A Global Survey on the Ambiguous State of Employee Trust," *Harvard Business Review*, July 22, 2016, https://hbr.org/2016/07/a-global-survey-on-the-ambiguous-state-of-employee-trust.

8   "4 Steps to Help Your Big Team Master the Art of Small Business Communication," Vocoli, October 8, 2015, https://www.vocoli.com/blog/october-2015/scaling-internal-communications/.

9   Amy Adkins, "Employee Engagement in U.S. Stagnant in 2015," *Gallup*, January 13, 2016, https://news.gallup.com/poll/188144/employee-engagement-stagnant-2015.aspx.

10 Charles Duhigg, "What Google Learned from Its Quest to Build the Perfect Team," *New York Times*, February 25, 2016, https://www.nytimes.com/2016/02/28/magazine/what-google-learned-from-its-quest-to-build-the-perfect-team.html.

11 "Can Relationships Boost Longevity and Well-Being?" Harvard Health Publishing, June 2017, https://www.health.harvard.edu/mental-health/can-relationships-boost-longevity-and-well-being.

12 Matthias R. Mehl, Simine Vazire, Shannon E. Holleran, and C. Shelby Clark, "Eavesdropping on Happiness: Well-Being Is Related to Having Less Small Talk and More Substantive Conversations," *Psychological Science* 21, no. 4 (2010), 539–41, https://journals.sagepub.com/doi/10.1177/0956797610362675.

13 John Bransford, et al., "Learning Theories and Education: Toward a Decade of Synergy," in *Handbook of Educational Psychology*, edited by P. Alexander and P. Winne (Mahwah, NJ: Elrbaum, 2006), 209–44, http://ilabs.washington.edu/kuhl/pdf/2006_Bransford_Vye_etal.pdf.

14 Bryant McGill, *Voice of Reason: Speaking to the Great and Good Spirit of Revolution of Mind* (Sarasota, FL: Paper Lyon, 2012).

15 Scott H. Frey and Valerie E. Gerry, "Modulation of Neural Activity During Observational Learning of Actions and Their Sequential Orders," *Journal of Neuroscience* 26, no. 51 (December 2006), 13194–201, https://www.cin.ucsf.edu/~houde/sensorimotor_jc /possible_papers/SHFrey06a.pdf.

16 Martin Fishbein, Harry C. Triandis, Frederick H. Kanfer, Marshall Becker, Susan E. Middlestadt, and Anita Eichler, "Factors Influencing Behavior and Behavior Change," in *Handbook of Educational Psychology*, edited by A. Baum, T. A. Revenson, and J. E. Singer (Mahwah, NJ: Elrbaum, 2001), 3–17, http://people.oregonstate. edu/~flayb/MY%20COURSES/H671%20Advanced%20Theory%20Winter16/Weekly /Fishbein%20etal01%20TheoristsConsensusConference.pdf.

17 Jamie Showkeir and Maren Showkeir, *Authentic Conversations: Moving from Manipulation to Truth and Commitment* (San Francisco: Berrett-Koehler, 2008).

18 Priya Parker, *The Art of Gathering: How We Meet and Why It Matters* (London: Penguin Business, 2019).

19 Juanita Brown, *The World Café Book: Shaping Our Futures through Conversations That Matter*, with David Isaacs (Berrett-Koehler Publishers: San Francisco, 2005).

20 Juanita Brown, David Isaacs, Eric Vogt, and Nancy Margulies, "Strategic Questions: Engaging People's Best Thinking," Systems Thinker, accessed August 12, 2019, https://thesystemsthinker.com/strategic-questions-engaging-peoples-best-thinking/.

21 Hyder Zahed, "The Power of Living With Daily Intentions," *HuffPost*, https://www .huffpost.com/entry/the-power-of-living-with-daily-intentions_b_8258444.

22 Oprah Winfrey, "The Power of Intention," *Super Soul Sunday*, video clip, 4:25, accessed September 11, 2019, http://www.oprah.com/own-super-soul-sunday/the-power-of -intention-video.

23 Brené Brown, *The Gifts of Imperfection: Let Go of Who You Think You're Supposed to Be and Embrace Who You Are* (Center City, MN: Hazelden, 2010).

24 Charles Duhigg, "What Google Learned from Its Quest to Build the Perfect Team."

25 John Bransford, et al., "Learning Theories and Education: Toward a Decade of Synergy."

26 "The Teacher is Talking: Kids Say the Darndest Things," Leslie Lindsay.

27 Michelle M. Chouinard, P. L. Harris, and Michael P. Maratsos, "Children's Questions: A Mechanism for Cognitive Development," *Monographs of the Society for Research in Child Development* 72, no. 1 (2007), i, v, vii–ix, 1–129, https://www.jstor.org/stable /pdf/30163594.pdf.

28 "Mothers Asked Nearly 300 Questions a Day, Study Finds," *The Telegraph*, March 28, 2013, https://www.telegraph.co.uk/news/uknews/9959026/Mothers-asked-nearly -300-questions-a-day-study-finds.html.

29 Warren Berger, "Why Curious People Are Destined for the C-Suite," *Harvard Business Review*, September 11, 2015, last modified October 7, 2016, https://hbr.org/2015/09 /why-curious-people-are-destined-for-the-c-suite.

30 Brian Grazer and Charles Fishman, *A Curious Mind: The Secret to a Bigger Life* (New York: Simon & Schuster, 2015), 188.

31 Matthias J. Gruber, Bernard D. Gelman, and Charan Ranganath, "States of Curiosity Modulate Hippocampus-Dependent Learning via the Dopaminergic Circuit," *Neuron* 84, no. 2 (October 2014), 486–96, https://www.ncbi.nlm.nih.gov/pmc/articles/ PMC4252494/.

32 "Naguib Mahfouz," *Wikiquote*, last modified October 2, 2016, https://en.wikiquote.org /wiki/Naguib_Mahfouz.

33 Kathleen S. Linehan and Ted L. Rosenthal, "Current Behavioral Approaches to Marital and Family Therapy," *Advances in Behavior Research and Therapy* 2, no. 3 (1979), 99–143, https://www.sciencedirect.com/science/article/pii/014664027990002X.

34 Stephen R. Covey, "Habit 5: Seek First to Understand, Then to Be Understood," Franklin Covey, https://www.franklincovey.com/the-7-habits/habit-5.html.

35 Lynn C. Miller, J. H. Berger, and R. L. Archer, "Openers: Individuals Who Elicit Intimate Self-Disclosure," *Journal of Personality and Social Psychology* 44, no. 6 (1983), 1234–44, https://psycnet.apa.org/record/1984-01323-001.

36 Karen Huang, Michael Yeomans, Alison Wood Brooks, Julia Minson, and Francesca Gino, "It Doesn't Hurt to Ask: Question-Asking Increases Liking," *Journal of Personality and Social Psychology* 113, no. 3 (2017), 430–52, https://www.hbs.edu/faculty /Publication%20Files/Huang%20et%20al%202017_6945bc5e-3b3e-4c0a-addd -254c9e603c60.pdf.

37 Harry T. Reis and Brian C. Patrick, "Attachment and Intimacy: Component Processes," in *Social Psychology: Handbook of Basic Principles*, edited by E. T. Higgins and A. W. Kruglanski (New York: Guilford Press, 1996), 523–63, https://psycnet.apa.org /record/1996-98402-018.

38 "Want to Know What Your Brain Does When It Hears a Question?" Decision Science News, February 21, 2017, https://www8.gsb.columbia.edu/decisionsciences /newsn/5051/want-to-know-what-your-brain-does-when-it-hears-a-question.

39 William Stringfellow, *Count It All Joy: Reflections on Faith, Doubt, and Temptation Seen Through the Letter of James* (Eugene, OR: Wipf & Stock, 1999), 16.

40 Ronald P. Carver, Raymond L. Johnson, and Herbert L. Friedman, "Factor Analysis of the Ability to Comprehend Time-Compressed Speech," Journal of Literacy Research 4, no. 1 (1971), 76–84, https://journals.sagepub.com/doi/abs/10.1080/10862967109546974.

41 Baltasar Gracian, *A Pocket Mirror for Heroes*, ed. and trans. Chrisopher Maurer (New York: Currency, 1996).

42 Stephan Getzmann, Julian Jasny, and Michael Falkenstein, "Switching of Auditory Attention in 'Cocktail-Party' Listening: ERP Evidence of Cueing Effects in Younger and Older Adults," *Brain and Cognition* 111 (2017), 1–12, https://www.ncbi.nlm.nih.gov /pubmed/27814564.

43 E. Colin Cherry, "Some Experiments on the Recognition of Speech, with One and with Two Ears," *The Journal of the Acoustical Society of America* 25, no. 5 (September 1953), 975–79, https://www.ee.columbia.edu/~dpwe/papers/Cherry53-cpe.pdf.

44 Henry David Thoreau, "Autumnal Tints," *The Atlantic*, October 1862, 385–402.

45 "Wait, Just a Second, Is Your Doctor Listening?" Springer Nature, July 19, 2018, https://www.springer.com/gp/about-springer/media/research-news/all-english -research-news/wait--just-a-second--is-your-doctor-listening-/15963052.

46 Molly McElroy, "While in Womb, Babies Begin Learning Language from Their Mothers," UW News, January 2, 2013, https://www.washington.edu/news/2013/01/02/while-in -womb-babies-begin-learning-language-from-their-mothers/.

47 Daniel Goleman, *Social Intelligence: The New Science of Human Relationships* (New York: Bantam, 2006), 54.

48 Mike Bagshaw, *Using Emotional Intelligence at Work: 17 Tried and Tested Activities for Understanding the Practical Applications of Emotional Intelligence* (Cambridgeshire, UK: Fenman, 2000), section 8.1.

49 Emily Teding van Berkhout and John M. Malouff, "The Efficacy of Empathy Training: A Meta-Analysis of Randomized Controlled Trials," *Journal of Counseling Psychology* 63, no. 1 (January 2016), 32–41, https://www.ncbi.nlm.nih.gov/pubmed/26191979.

50 Jason Marsh, "Do Mirror Neurons Give Us Empathy?" *Greater Good Magazine*, March 29, 2012, https://greatergood.berkeley.edu/article/item/do_mirror_neurons_give_empathy.

51 John Payton, Roger P. Weissberg, Joseph A. Durlak, Allison B. Dymnicki, Rebecca D. Taylor, Kristen B. Shellinger, and Molly Pachan, *The Positive Impact of Social and Emotional Learning for Kindergarten to Eighth-Grade Students: Findings from Three Scientific Reviews* (Chicago: Collaborative for Academic, Social, and Emotional Learning, 2008), https://www.casel.org/wp-content/uploads/2016/08/PDF-4-the-positive-impact-of-social-and-emotional-learning-for-kindergarten-to-eighth-grade-students-executive-summary.pdf.

52 "Empathy and Cooperation Go Hand in Hand," Neuroscience News, April 9, 2019, https://neurosciencenews.com/empathy-cooperation-11047/.

53 Don Miguel Ruiz, *The Four Agreements: A Practical Guide to Personal Freedom* (Carlsbad, CA: Amber-Allen, 1997).

54 Source unknown. Alfred Brendel is a classical musician.

55 Dennis Abrams, *Sandra Day O'Connor: U.S. Supreme Court Justice* (New York: Chelsea House, 2009), 41.

56 "Ramana Pemmaraju," *Goodreads*, accessed February 8, 2017, https://www.goodreads.com/author/quotes/14045201.Ramana_Pemmaraju.

57 "Quotes About Talker," *Goodreads*, accessed February 8, 2017, http://www.goodreads.com/quotes/tag/talker.

58 Christopher Uhl, "Steering Into the Curve: Getting Real in the Classroom," *College Teaching* 58, no. 3 (2010): 107, http://web.a.ebscohost.com.res.banq.qc.ca/ehost/pdfviewer/pdfviewer?vid=2&sid=2a42c258-33bc-4ac6-bce3-6e891a7c4254%40sessionmgr4009&hid=4209.

59 Joseph P. Lash, *Helen and Teacher: The Story of Helen Keller and Anne Sullivan Macy* (New York: Merloyd Lawrence, 1980).

60 Walter Sullivan, "The Einstein Papers. A Man of Many Parts," *New York Times*, March 29, 1972, accessed March 8, 2017, http://www.nytimes.com/1972/03/29/archives/the-einstein-papers-a-man-of-many-parts-the-einstein-papers-man-of.html?_r=0.

WiLL WiSE, MEd

Cofounder and Chief Weologist at We and Me Inc.

Photo credit to Trish Hummer

Will Wise has been asking powerful questions for over two decades as a corporate development consultant, nontraditional school principal, university instructor, and team development thought leader. Will is also the cofounder of We and Me Inc. (www.weand.me), a company who partners with leaders and organizations to transform workplaces by establishing a culture of connection to save them time, increase productivity, and boost job satisfaction. He works with leaders to develop *who they are*—not just what they do. Will's clients have included JetBlue, TEDx, Typeform, NBC Universal, Penn State, and many others. He lives in Central Pennsylvania with his wife and three children.

CHAD LiTTLEFiELD, MEd

Cofounder and Chief Experience Officer at We and Me Inc.

Photo credit to Erica Mueller

As a global keynote speaker and expert facilitator, Chad designs experiences and tools that build trust, strengthen connections, and unify your team. He helps break down communication barriers to make teams more cohesive, effective, and higher performing. He is a TEDx speaker and is also the author of the *Pocket Guide to Facilitating Human Connections*. He and Will are the cocreators of *We! Connect Cards*™, which are now being used to create conversations that matter within companies in over eighty countries around the world and on six of the seven continents. (Free deck if you live in Antarctica.) Chad lives in Pittsburgh, PA, with his wife and son, Kate and Otto, though they travel often for business and adventure.

Follow Will and Chad to receive actionable insights through their free interactive learning letter read by thousands of top leaders right here:

www.weand.me/ideas

About *We and Me Inc.*™

Hi!

Will Wise and Chad Littlefield here to share a bit about our company, *We and Me Inc.*™ Our mission and passion is to *create conversations that matter*.

We are mildly obsessed with relationships, group dynamics, learning and development, connection, and team performance. We design and deliver trainings, programs, and keynotes that actually work. And we've got the data to prove it. We'd be happy to share our success stories, whether helping tech startups like Typeform.com or Fortune 500 companies like JetBlue.

We believe . . .

- Leaders accomplish more by asking powerful questions than by commanding and controlling.
- Deeper human connection fosters more engagement and better performance.
- People, purpose, and planet are just as important as profit.
- Interactive experiences have more impact than PowerPoint slides because people learn by doing.

Not only do we believe these things, but we are genuinely excited about making them a reality for each organization we work with.

View our services on the next page and get in touch to explore working with Will Wise and *We and Me Inc.*™

Let us help get *your* team working better together.

Invite us to . . .

Speak at your conference
or large-audience event.

▸ Create deeper connections
and meaning-filled
interactions, resulting in
communities rather than
fragmented groups.

Run a **custom company retreat** and dive deep.

▸ Build relationships that
inspire employees to stay.
▸ Strengthen the culture for
your workplace.

Run **on-site workshops at your place of work**, with
a focus on developing your
leaders.

▸ Learn skills and leave with
concrete tools to navigate
difficult conversations.

Contact us to explore availability, pricing, and working together.

www.weand.me   hello@weand.me

CPSIA information can be obtained
at www.ICGtesting.com
Printed in the USA
LVHW020855080921
697193LV00012B/1091